The Cambridge Introduction to
Joseph Conrad

Joseph Conrad is one of the most intriguing and important modernist novelists. His writing continues to preoccupy twenty-first-century readers. This introduction by a leading scholar is aimed at students coming to Conrad's work for the first time. The rise of postcolonial studies has inspired new interest in Conrad's themes of travel, exploration, and racial and ethnic conflict. John Peters explains how these themes are explored in his major works, *Nostromo, Lord Jim*, and "Heart of Darkness" as well as his shorter stories. He provides an essential overview of Conrad's fascinating life and career and his approach to writing and literature. A guide to further reading is included, which points to some of the most useful secondary criticism on Conrad. This is the most comprehensive and concise introduction to studying Conrad available, and it will be essential reading for students of the twentieth-century novel and of modernism.

JOHN G. PETERS is Associate Professor of English at the University of North Texas.

Cambridge Introductions to Literature

This series is designed to introduce students to key topics and authors. Accessible and lively, these introductions will also appeal to readers who want to broaden their understanding of the books and authors they enjoy.

- Ideal for students, teachers, and lecturers
- Concise, yet packed with essential information
- Key suggestions for further reading

Titles in this series:

The Cambridge Introduction to
Joseph Conrad

JOHN G. PETERS

CAMBRIDGE
UNIVERSITY PRESS

CAMBRIDGE UNIVERSITY PRESS
Cambridge, New York, Melbourne, Madrid, Cape Town, Singapore, São Paulo

CAMBRIDGE UNIVERSITY PRESS
The Edinburgh Building, Cambridge CB2 2RU, UK
Published in the United States of America by Cambridge University Press, New York

www.cambridge.org
Information on this title: www.cambridge.org/9780521548670

© John G. Peters 2006

First published 2006

Printed in the United Kingdom at the University Press, Cambridge

A catalogue record for this book is available from the British Library

ISBN-13 978-0-521-83972-3 hardback
ISBN-10 0-521-83972-6 hardback
ISBN-13 978-0-521-54867-0 paperback
ISBN-10 0-521-54867-5 paperback

For my grandfather, George L. Snider, and my late grandmother, Ruth E. Snider

Contents

Preface

This book is intended as a general overview of the life, works, and context of Joseph Conrad. I hope that this study will be of use to both students and scholars of Conrad, as well as to the interested non-specialist. The book begins with Conrad's life (particularly in relation to his writings), then moves to the context in which he wrote, then considers Conrad's fiction, and concludes with the critical reception of Conrad's works. In the process, I have necessarily had to narrow my discussion to the most essential points. I would have liked to have discussed Conrad's non-fiction prose, but there simply was not space enough to do so. In my discussion of Conrad's works, I have included, of course, my own thoughts on them, but I have also included standard views of these works so that the newcomer to Conrad's works will have access to a wide-ranging discussion.

Unlike most overviews I have considered all of Conrad's published fiction except *The Sisters*, the novel fragment that he abandoned some twenty-five years or more before his death. I have also not considered the three works upon which Conrad collaborated with Ford Madox Ford (*The Inheritors, Romance*, and *The Nature of the Crime*) because these books were largely Ford's work. On the other hand, I have commented on every other fictional work Conrad wrote, including the stories collected in the posthumous *Tales of Hearsay*, all of which were finished during Conrad's lifetime, and the posthumous unfinished novel *Suspense*. Unlike most overviews of Conrad's works, I have not dismissed his less studied stories and novels but rather have focused on such aspects of those works that I believe to be worth considering. As a result, I hope that the student of Conrad will come away with a better feel for Conrad's entire career, not just for his middle career for which he is best known. At the same time, however, I have spent the bulk of my effort on the works of Conrad's middle period. In considering all of Conrad's fiction works while emphasizing those of his middle period, I hope I have presented a balanced and useful view of Conrad's works and career.

In quoting from Conrad's works, I have used the uniform 1928 Doubleday edition, with the exception of *The Secret Agent*, where I have quoted from The Cambridge Edition of the Works of Joseph Conrad version of the novel, edited by Bruce Harkness and S. W. Reid.

Acknowledgments

I would like to thank Dr. Ray Ryan of Cambridge University Press for his helpful suggestions in preparing this book; various colleagues including Gene Moore, Susan Jones, Keith Carabine, Peter Lancelot Mallios, Zdzisław Najder, Laurence Davies, Andrea White, Carola Kaplan, Martin Bock, Sid Reid, John McClure, Hunt Hawkins, Brian Richardson, and many others (too many to count) who have been kind enough to share their knowledge of Conrad with me and thus improve my understanding of him and his works; and my colleagues in the Department of English at the University of North Texas, particularly David Holdeman, Bruce Bond, and Scott Simpkins, for their support of my work. I am also grateful to the Office of the Vice President of Research at the University of North Texas for their support in the form of grants that have helped in completing this book. Finally, I would like to express my appreciation to my family, my grandfather George Snider, my mother Virginia Long, my aunt Ruth Snider, and especially my daughter Kaitlynne and my wife Deanna for their support, encouragement, and patience.

Chapter 1

Conrad's life

Józef Teodor Konrad Korzeniowski was born in Berdyczów in a predominantly Polish part of Ukraine on December 3, 1857 to Apollo Korzeniowski and his wife Ewelina Bobrowska. Conrad's parents were of the *szlachta*, the Polish gentry. At the time of Conrad's birth, Poland had been partitioned among Prussia, Russia, and Austria-Hungary for over sixty years. Apollo Korzeniowski was a writer and a man passionately committed to Polish independence. He played a prominent role in the revolutionary activities of the early 1860s, for which he was arrested and convicted of seditious actions. In 1862, Korzeniowski was sentenced to exile and sent to Vologda, Russia, and then later to Chernikhov. He was accompanied by his wife and young son, and the family suffered greatly during their exile. As a result of the poor conditions, Conrad's parents both contracted tuberculosis, and his mother died in April 1865. This was a solitary time in Conrad's life, as the boy spent most of his time in the sole company of his father. Korzeniowski remained in exile until early 1868 when he was allowed to leave in order to aid in Conrad's recovery from an illness. This was a better time for them, but Korzeniowski's tuberculosis soon worsened, and he died in May of 1869, leaving Conrad an orphan. Korzeniowski was given a hero's burial and is still considered a national hero in Poland.

Conrad's experience with his father during their time together very much influenced his later years. His devotion to literature, interest in revolutionary politics, attitudes about Russia, skeptical view of the world, and sometimes adventurous spirit all probably have some origin in his experience with his father. After his father's death, Conrad was cared for by family and friends, particularly Tadeusz Bobrowski, his maternal uncle, who became a second father to Conrad. Unlike the fiery and idealistic Korzeniowski, Bobrowski was conservative, careful, practical, and ultimately disapproving of Korzeniowski's approach to the world. Over the years, Bobrowski exerted a strong influence on Conrad and his attitudes, so Conrad's character seems to have been very much affected by both his father and his uncle.

As early as 1872, Conrad expressed a desire to pursue a life at sea. This was an unusual career choice for a Polish boy, and Conrad was certainly influenced in his choice by his reading of such authors as Cooper and Marryat. In 1874, Bobrowski finally agreed to allow Conrad to move to Marseilles, France, to pursue his maritime training. Thus at age seventeen, Conrad in effect left Poland for good. In Marseilles, Conrad studied his trade, and his uncle supported him with a generous allowance, but as Bobrowski's letters attest, Conrad was irresponsible with money, and although Bobrowski always rescued Conrad from his youthful irresponsibility, he constantly upbraided him for such failings.

In July of 1876, Conrad served as a steward aboard the *Saint Antoine*, which traveled to the Carribean and the Americas, and this represents Conrad's only experience in the new world. It would prove to be the basis for his most panoramic novel, *Nostromo*. Later, in early 1878, Conrad apparently went through a good deal of money, may have been involved in a romantic encounter (possibly with the model for Doña Rita of *The Arrow of Gold*), and may have been involved in some smuggling activity. What occurred after this time is not entirely clear, but, according to Bobrowski's letters, it appears that Conrad attempted suicide. The event remains obscure because at the time and in later years Conrad claimed to have been wounded in a duel.

During these years, the issue of Conrad's citizenship became increasingly important. Bobrowski agreed to allow Conrad to go to Marseilles not only because of Conrad's desire to pursue a life at sea, but because, as a result of his father's revolutionary activities, Conrad was subject to lengthy conscription in the Russian army. Bobrowski thought that by moving to France, Conrad could become naturalized in another country more easily. Because France required a valid passport to work in the French Merchant Marine Service, however, and because Russia refused to issue such a passport to Conrad, it became clear that Conrad would not be free from military obligations to Russia if he remained in France. Consequently, Bobrowski encouraged Conrad to seek naturalization elsewhere. Thus, Conrad eventually joined the British Merchant Marine service, despite speaking no English at that time.

Over the next few years, Conrad sailed on several English ships, and in 1880 he studied to become an officer, passed his examination, and shortly thereafter became third mate aboard the *Loch Etive*. Wishing to move up the professional ladder, Conrad went in search of a position as second mate, finally obtaining one aboard the *Palestine* in November 1881. His experience aboard the *Palestine* was to become the raw material for one of his most important short stories, "Youth." A good deal of Conrad's experience aboard the *Palestine* resembles the events chronicled in "Youth," including the lengthy repairs before finally setting out, the ship catching fire, their experience in life boats, and Conrad's first close-up view of the exotic East.

Conrad continued to ply his trade, and in 1884 found himself ashore in Bombay, India, where he accepted a position as second mate aboard the *Narcissus*. His experience was to form the basis for his first great novel *The Nigger of the "Narcissus."* Upon arriving in England again, Conrad had completed the required time to qualify for the first officer examination. After some initial difficulty, he eventually passed the examination. However, positions were scarce, and, unable to obtain a position as first officer, despite his new certificate, Conrad finally accepted one as second officer aboard the *Tilkhurst* in April 1885. In 1886, Conrad took the examination for a master's certificate, which would qualify him to serve as captain, but failed one section. In July, Conrad applied for British naturalization and was formally accepted on August 18, and later that year Conrad again took the master's examination, this time passing it. In 1887, Conrad shipped out of Singapore as first mate aboard the *Vidar*, which stopped in various ports throughout the Malay Archipelago. Conrad's time aboard the *Vidar* was his first opportunity to experience the East for an extended period of time, and the experience would become valuable material for much of his fiction about the East. In January 1888, Conrad left the *Vidar* and shortly thereafter received his first and only command when he was appointed captain of the *Otago*. This experience would provide the basis for much of Conrad's fiction, particularly *The Shadow-Line*, "Falk," "A Smile of Fortune," and "The Secret Sharer." The *Otago* was based out of Australia, and during his time in command, Conrad traveled to Port Louis, Mauritius, as well as to various ports along the Australian coast. In March 1889, Conrad decided to give up command of the *Otago*. The reasons for this decision have remained a mystery. He may have been averse to living in the East on a relatively permanent basis, or he may have harbored thoughts of eventually pursuing a career on land in England. Shortly afterwards, a significant change occurred in Conrad's life: he began to write his first novel, *Almayer's Folly* – in English. He could have written in Polish or French, but chose English instead.

Having been unsuccessful in finding a berth bound for the East, Conrad began looking for a command in Africa. He went to Brussels and met Albert Thys, the director of the *Société Belge pour le Commerce du Haut-Congo*, about the possibility of commanding a steamboat on the Congo River. While there, Conrad met a distant relative, Aleksander Poradowski, and his wife, Marguerite. Poradowski died only days after Conrad met him, but the visit was fortuitous in that Conrad and Marguerite became close friends. Shortly before leaving for the Congo, Conrad made his first trip home to Poland in sixteen years. With experiences so different from those he encountered, Conrad was uncomfortable and must have recognized how little he had in common by then with his compatriots.

In May 1890, Conrad set off on one of the most important voyages of his life when he traveled to the Congo to accept his post. His experience would be recorded in part in his "Congo Diary," but it would also become the basis for "An Outpost of Progress" and his most widely known tale "Heart of Darkness." He arrived on the Congo River in June and began his journey up river, proceeding from Bowa to Matadi. During his stay, he became friendly with Roger Casement, who later became famous when he exposed the atrocities occurring in the Belgian Congo. Despite the colonial enterprise being depicted in Europe as a humanitarian endeavor, Conrad found a great deal of greed, waste, and chaos. In early August, Conrad arrived in Kinshasa intent on taking command of the steamboat *Florida*. The *Florida*, however, had been damaged, and Conrad instead had to travel up river on the *Roi des Belges*, under the command of another captain. They arrived at Stanley Falls (now Kisangani) at the beginning of September and shortly thereafter headed back to Kinshasa. Conrad was asked to take over command of the *Roi des Belges* temporarily while the captain was ill, and the few days he acted as substitute captain constitute Conrad's only command in Africa. The return voyage carried a sick agent, George Antoine Klein, who died on route. Klein became one of the models for Kurtz in "Heart of Darkness." During the next several months, Conrad traveled throughout the Congo on company business and appears to have suffered a good deal from ill health, so much so that he was eventually invalided home, arriving back in Europe at the end of January 1891. Conrad's experience in the Congo had an enormous impact on him. Despite its relative brevity, it would affect him for the rest of his life and as much as anything else influenced his outlook on civilization and human existence itself. His criticism of the abuses and disorder he witnessed was unrelenting, as evidenced in his various writings on the subject.

After returning from the Congo, Conrad spent some months recovering his physical and psychological health. In November of 1891, he accepted a first mate position aboard the *Torrens*, which regularly sailed between England and Australia. On a return trip from Australia in March 1893, Conrad met Edward Lancelot Sanderson and John Galsworthy, who would become Conrad's life-long friends. Both would also become literary figures, Galsworthy an important novelist and playwright, and Sanderson a minor poet. In July, the *Torrens* arrived in England, and Conrad decided to resign his position and take an extended trip to Poland. By late 1893, he was back in

England and looking for work. He signed on to the steamer *Adowa* in late November and sailed to Rouen, France, intending to carry passengers to Canada, but the trip never materialized, and so in January the *Adowa* returned to London. Although he didn't know it at the time, when Conrad disembarked he left his life at sea behind him for ever. The next month, another dramatic change occurred in Conrad's life when Tadeusz Bobrowski died, leaving a spiritual void in Conrad's life. Despite their different temperaments, Bobrowski's influence on Conrad had been unmistakable, and Conrad keenly felt his uncle's loss.

Although Conrad continued to look for work at sea, he was unsuccessful and was already beginning his journey toward a new life. Throughout the first half of 1894, he worked to finish *Almayer's Folly*, which he sent to T. Fisher Unwin in early July. Then in August, Conrad began what he thought would be a short story entitled "Two Vagabonds," but, as was to happen frequently in his career, the story evolved into a full-length novel, *An Outcast of the Islands*. In early October, Unwin agreed to publish *Almayer's Folly* and Conrad officially began his literary career. The acceptance of *Almayer's Folly* also brought Conrad in touch with one of his most important literary contacts: Edward Garnett. Garnett was one of Unwin's readers and had recommended the book to him. Conrad soon developed a close friendship with Garnett, and much of his most interesting correspondence is with Garnett. More important than the personal friendship, however, was Garnett's eye for good literature, and he became an invaluable sounding board for Conrad's future writings, as well as being instrumental in introducing Conrad to a number of important people.

Almayer's Folly took longer to write than most of Conrad's other works, but he seemed to suffer from none of the emotional stress and depression that would so mark his literary career. As early as *An Outcast of the Islands*, though, Conrad was beset with self doubt and depression about his work, and, as would prove to be the case almost invariably, Conrad struggled mightily with its writing. While Conrad was still wrestling with *An Outcast of the Islands*, *Almayer's Folly* appeared in print in early 1895. The reviews were generally positive, and Conrad was pleased, but despite the positive reviews, the book did not sell well. His experience with *Almayer's Folly* would be one with which he would soon become familiar. For nearly the first twenty years of his writing career, reviews of Conrad's books generally would be overwhelmingly favorable, but his books would not sell. This cycle of agonized writing, followed by positive reception, followed by poor sales would contribute to Conrad's constant problems with health and finances. Conrad finished *An Outcast of the Islands* in September of 1895, and shortly after completing it began a third novel, entitled *The Sisters*. He worked on it for several months, sending part of the manuscript to Garnett for evaluation. Based on Garnett's comments and on his own opinion, Conrad eventually abandoned the project around March of 1896.

About this time a significant change occurred in Conrad's life. Little is known regarding his courtship of Jessie George, a typist, whom he appears to have met perhaps as early as 1894. Jessie came from humble origins, but apparently, as they worked together, an intimacy evolved. All that can be said for certain is that their relationship developed quickly, and by March 24, 1896 Conrad was a married man. Conrad's choice of Jessie has puzzled many. Coming from such different backgrounds, the pair would seem to have been ill suited for one another. Apparently, Conrad did not even find Jessie particularly attractive. Nevertheless, despite their differences, their marriage appears to have been reasonably successful. Perhaps only someone of Jesse's temperament could have dealt with someone of Conrad's temperament. In any case, their marriage worked out better than most probably would have predicted. The couple honeymooned in Brittany, during which time Conrad wrote the short story "The Idiots." Having abandoned *The Sisters*, Conrad turned his attention to what would become his most difficult novel project: *The Rescuer* (later titled *The Rescue*). Begun in 1896, the novel was some twenty-three years in its completion.

While struggling with *The Rescuer*, Conrad continued to work on other projects. During this time, he wrote perhaps the best of his early stories, "An Outpost of Progress." Conrad also wrote "The Lagoon" and probably began work on *The Nigger of the "Narcissus."* Reviews of *An Outcast of the Islands* also began to come out about this time, and, like those of *Almayer's Folly*, they were generally favorable. As it turns out, one of the reviewers was H. G. Wells, with whom Conrad corresponded. This resulted in a friendship that lasted for a number of years before they had a falling out.

Conrad's poor management of money became a problem once again as he lost a good deal of his inheritance from Bobrowski through speculative investing. This situation would be the beginning of the constant financial difficulties that would beset Conrad for at least the next fifteen years. Conrad and Jesse returned to England in September and settled into their new life. Conrad soon began working in earnest on *The Nigger of the "Narcissus,"* one of the few novels over which he did not seem to struggle. He finished it in January of 1897; it was to be Conrad's first literary masterpiece and the one which would initiate his most productive literary period. In February, Conrad made another important literary friendship, this time with Henry James. Conrad thought James to be the greatest living novelist, and in turn

James appreciated Conrad's work. Around this time, Conrad also began writing "Karain," which he thought would be easy and bring in some money if placed in a good magazine. The story turned out to be more difficult than he expected, and Garnett's advice and help placing the story were invaluable, particularly since the story was eventually published in *Blackwood's Magazine*, one of the premier magazines of the day. Whilst writing "Karain," Conrad began work on "The Return." This long story cost Conrad considerable effort but was one of his more disappointing efforts. It was one of only two stories that Conrad was never able to place in a magazine.

In August 1897, an important and interesting acquaintance entered Conrad's life. After reading "An Outpost of Progress," R. B. Cunninghame Graham wrote to Conrad expressing his admiration for the story. Graham remained a friend to Conrad for the rest of Conrad's life. In some ways similar and in some ways different, the two made an interesting pair. Graham was a swashbuckling figure and descended from the Scottish aristocracy. Some of Conrad's most significant letters were written to Graham, and Graham was a useful sounding board for Conrad's political and literary views. Conrad seems to have been able to be more direct with Graham than he was with others, and Conrad's view of the world and his pervasive skepticism are particularly pronounced in many of his letters to him.

During the summer of 1897, Conrad wrote his most important statement of aesthetic theory when he composed a preface to *The Nigger of the "Narcissus."* About this time, Conrad was introduced to Stephen Crane, who had been impressed with *The Nigger of the "Narcissus"* and wanted to meet Conrad. The two developed a strong friendship that was cut short by Crane's untimely death. Conrad genuinely appreciated much of what Crane wrote and certainly appreciated his warm friendship. Throughout this time, *The Rescue* hung over Conrad's head. Although still intending to complete the novel, he made little headway. Meanwhile, *The Nigger of the "Narcissus"* appeared in book form in early December and was Conrad's most successful book to that point, receiving even more favorable reviews than had his previous novels. Unfortunately, once again, praise did not translate into significant sales, and Conrad's financial situation grew steadily worse.

In January of 1898, Conrad's first son, Borys, was born. Though slow to take to the idea of fatherhood, Conrad eventually developed a warm relationship with both of his sons. In March, he published his first story collection entitled *Tales of Unrest*, which contained "Karain," "The Idiots," "An Outpost of Progress," "The Return," and "The Lagoon." Although *The Rescue* was supposed to be Conrad's primary focus at this time, he continued to work on other projects. It was during this time that Conrad wrote "Youth."

The story first introduces Conrad's readers to his most famous character, Charlie Marlow. Marlow narrates "Youth," as he does "Heart of Darkness" and *Lord Jim* shortly thereafter. Many years later, Marlow would take his curtain call as narrator of *Chance*.

Conrad's financial situation continued to deteriorate, both because of his inability to finish *The Rescue* and because of his habit of living beyond his means. In October, Conrad moved to Pent Farm in Kent, renting a cottage from Ford Madox Ford (Hueffer), to whom Garnett had introduced him. Although Conrad had closer long-term friendships and longer literary relationships, none were probably as important to his development as a writer as was his relationship with Ford. The two writers even collaborated on three projects: *The Inheritors, Romance,* and *The Nature of the Crime*. Their theories about literature and literary techniques tended to rub off on one another, and for many years the two were close friends. Ford probably got more out of this literary relationship than did Conrad, but it would be wrong to assume that Conrad learned nothing from Ford.

Probably around June of 1898, Conrad began working on *Lord Jim*, which he had assumed would be a short story. In the fall, he began working on the piece in earnest, and in December, while working on *Lord Jim*, Conrad began "Heart of Darkness," which later appeared in *Blackwood's Magazine*. Compared to his usual experience, Conrad had little trouble writing "Heart of Darkness" and in a relatively short time produced one of his finest works. In January, Conrad received a prize from the literary weekly *Academy* for *Tales of Unrest*. Despite his increased critical acclaim, however, Conrad's financial circumstances were no better.

In February, the publishers dropped plans to bring out *The Rescue*, and Conrad was relieved of a weighty burden. In the meantime, he continued to work on *Lord Jim*. Around this time, Conrad unknowingly became embroiled in a painful episode. Wincenty Lutosławski, having met Conrad some time earlier, wrote an article entitled "The Emigration of Talent," in which he either misunderstood or misrepresented Conrad to be an example of an ex-patriot Pole who chose to write in English rather than Polish because of the greater financial possibilities. The article resulted in Eliza Orzeszkowa's scathing attack on Conrad, in which she accused him of selling out and betraying Poland. When Conrad learned of this exchange he was both hurt and angered. This would not be the only time that Conrad would be made to feel that he had betrayed Poland by leaving his homeland. Conrad was particularly sensitive to such criticism and probably did feel some guilt over having left.

Meanwhile, the first installment of *Lord Jim* appeared in the October issue of *Blackwood's Magazine*. At various points, Conrad thought the novel was nearing its conclusion, but each time he would be wrong. At this time, he was working almost exclusively on the novel, but he did break away on occasion to collaborate with Ford on *The Inheritors*. As with all of their collaborative works, although Conrad made significant contributions, for the most part the work represents Ford's ideas, work, and writing. Also in October, the Second Boer War had broken out, and Conrad first revealed his extreme skepticism toward politics. Although he felt an allegiance toward his adopted country, he was, at the same time, extremely suspicious of politics and jingoism.

In the meantime, Conrad continued to experience difficulties writing *Lord Jim*, while financial and health troubles also plagued him. Nevertheless, he made good progress on the novel. During this time, Crane's illness took a turn for the worse, and Conrad saw him for the last time in May, shortly before Crane died. Crane was a good friend to Conrad, and Conrad's affection for Crane's memory never wavered.

The next month would bring an end to *Lord Jim* and to the novel that many believe to be his greatest. After finally finishing *Lord Jim*, Conrad next began working with Ford on a collaborative novel entitled *Seraphina* (later *Romance*). About this time, Conrad accepted an offer from James B. Pinker to act as Conrad's literary agent. This arrangement relieved Conrad of the trouble of finding places in which to publish his work and also provided him with a more regular income. Although their relationship was at times volatile, Pinker was a great supporter of Conrad and made his life easier. In late 1900, *Lord Jim* appeared in book form, and again reviews were quite positive. However, as the novel was the first work that fully implemented Conrad's narrative experimentations, reviewers also expressed a good deal of confusion. Strong praise of the novel from Henry James, though, greatly pleased Conrad. Again, sales were modest, and Conrad's financial difficulties continued. By September, Conrad had begun his next important story, "Typhoon," which he finished in January of 1901. He then began work on "Falk," the only story besides "The Return" that he was unable to publish in serial form. Unlike "The Return," whose difficulty may have been its quality, the difficulty with "Falk" appears to have been its subject material, in which cannibalism appears prominently. The story was finished in April, and, like "The Return," eventually found its way into a collection of stories.

With "Falk" completed, Conrad and Ford began working in greater earnest on *Romance* and Conrad continued to work on his own writings, composing "Amy Foster" during part of May and June of 1901. In June, while Conrad and Ford were working on *Romance*, *The Inheritors* was published. *The Inheritors* did not sell well and, unlike Conrad's own books, it was not very favorably reviewed, either. Conrad and Ford worked on *Romance* through the summer and fall of 1901. In the fall, Conrad also began his story "To-morrow," which he finished in February 1902. Early in 1902, Conrad and Ford were still working on *Romance*. Unfortunately, they were unable to get it serialized, at which point Conrad turned his attention to "The End of the Tether."

In the midst of deep financial difficulties, Conrad experienced yet another set back when part of the manuscript for "The End of the Tether" was burned when a lamp exploded. In July, though, Conrad received some good news in the form of a grant from the Royal Literary Society, which helped to alleviate some of his financial difficulties. The next few months were spent primarily in completing "The End of the Tether." In November, Conrad and Ford again took up *Romance*, and at the same time "*Youth*" *and Two Other Stories* (which included "Youth," "Heart of Darkness," and "The End of the Tether") appeared to somewhat more mixed reviews. However, the book sold a little better than his previous books. November also brought the beginning of Conrad's next important work: *Nostromo*. Unlike Conrad's previous writings, which were drawn largely from personal experience, *Nostromo* came almost exclusively from Conrad's imagination and his reading. The novel would grow and grow, and much of Conrad's writing in 1903 was spent on it.

In April, "*Typhoon*" *and Other Stories* (containing "Typhoon," "Amy Foster," "Falk," and "To-morrow") appeared and was well received, and in September, Conrad was forced to set aside *Nostromo* in order to complete the final work on *Romance*, which was finally published in October. The novel's reception was not particularly good, and it did not bring the authors the popularity they desired. Conrad then returned to *Nostromo*, finding the task incredibly difficult and often a cause of bouts of illness and depression. In January 1904, *Nostromo* began to be serialized, and in the same month Conrad also began writing some non-fiction sketches of his life at sea. Eventually, these would become part of *The Mirror of the Sea*. Shortly thereafter, while still working on *Nostromo*, Conrad began writing a stage version of "To-morrow," entitled *One More Day*.

The difficult work on *Nostromo* continued, while Conrad also wrote more sketches for *The Mirror of the Sea*. This latter book seems to have emerged in part at Ford's instigation and perhaps also through Ford's help in that Ford apparently made suggestions, asked questions, and generally helped in the book's construction. Meanwhile, Conrad's financial difficulties continued, but William Rothenstein, a well-known portrait painter, had become friendly with Conrad and helped to arrange for a loan that greatly helped the situation. Finally, at the end of August, Conrad finished *Nostromo*. Given the novel's complexity and difficulty, it is not surprising that it was, with a few notable exceptions, misunderstood and not very favorably reviewed. Sales of the book were correspondingly modest.

After completing *Nostromo*, Conrad seems to have found it difficult to write. In November, he began work on what would become "Gaspar Ruiz," which appears to have been little more than an attempt to write a popular story for money. During that time, Conrad also wrote more sketches for *The Mirror of the Sea*. For some time, Jessie had been suffering from a knee injury. Her condition, along with his feeling of writer's block, prompted Conrad to plan a trip to Capri as a restorative vacation. It was in Capri that Conrad wrote his most famous political essay: "Autocracy and War," in which he expounded his views, particularly those regarding Russia.

Conrad's financial difficulties were alleviated for a time when he received a grant (largely through Rothenstein's intervention) from the Royal Bounty fund. He returned to England, and in June 1905 *One More Day* was performed. Although two important drama critics, Max Beerbohm and George Bernard Shaw, both liked the play, it did not result in the financial success for which Conrad had hoped. During the summer of 1905, Conrad wrote two more essays for *The Mirror of the Sea*, as well as his essay "Books," a further statement of his views on writing. In the fall, he wrote more sketches for *The Mirror of the Sea*, finished "Gaspar Ruiz," and began working on what would eventually become *Chance* – one of Conrad's more drawn-out novel projects, although not to the degree of *The Rescue*. Later in the fall of 1905, Conrad produced rather quickly "The Brute," "The Anarchist," and "The Informer." The latter two demonstrate his continuing interest in political issues and serve as precursors to the issues he would investigate in *The Secret Agent* and *Under Western Eyes*. In February 1906, Conrad again decided to go abroad, this time to southern France, and began work on "Verloc," another story that would eventually grow into a novel (*The Secret Agent*). The essays for *The Mirror of the Sea* were now complete, and Conrad began preparing the book for publication.

Conrad returned to England in April and around that time again collaborated with Ford, this time on *The Nature of the Crime*, a novella, which again was aimed at a popular audience. As before, Ford did the bulk of the writing, and the work later appeared in *The English Review*. In August, Conrad welcomed the birth of his second son, John, named after John Galsworthy, and in October, *The Mirror of the Sea* was published and well received. Wells, Kipling, Galsworthy, and Henry James all wrote favorable reviews, but the book did not sell very well. All this time, Conrad had also been working on *The Secret Agent*, completing it in November. While writing the novel, Conrad experienced few of his usual difficulties. After completing it, however, Conrad, as he did so often, fell into depression. After finishing most of his important works, his emotional and psychological energy would give out, as if the concentrated strain of creative production would finally release once the project was finished.

Conrad's next project was his short story "Il Conde," which he finished in December and followed with another trip to the south of France. The setting proved particularly conducive to Conrad's already strong interest in Napoleonic France, and he spent several months writing "The Duel." In May, the family went to Switzerland, in part because of Borys's health problems. Conrad returned to England in August and shortly afterwards moved from Pent Farm to Someries in Bedford. In September 1907, *The Secret Agent* was published in book form and, like *Nostromo*, was misunderstood. Although some reviews were positive, more were negative, and, not surprisingly, the book sold poorly. All this time, Conrad was supposed to be writing *Chance*, but he made little progress. Instead, in December 1907, he began work on what he thought would be another short story entitled "Razumov," but which was to evolve into *Under Western Eyes*, and consequently Conrad laid *Chance* aside again. In early 1908, he completed "The Black Mate," which was primarily an attempt to bring in a little money. The bulk of Conrad's time, however, was spent working on *Under Western Eyes*. Unlike *The Secret Agent*, the new novel was slow and difficult work for him, perhaps unsurprisingly, since the book is about Russia and revolutionary politics.

In August, another collection of Conrad's stories was published: *A Set of Six*, containing "Gaspar Ruiz," "The Informer," "The Brute," "The Anarchist," "The Duel," and "Il Conde." Lacking most of the narrative difficulties of Conrad's most recent novels, the collection was well received. About this time, Conrad also began what would become *A Personal Record*. Again, the idea for the volume may have come first from Ford. In any case, Ford was a strong advocate of the book, and when he started his important journal, *The English Review*, a selection appeared in the first issue and was later followed by other selections. The year 1909 also marked the downfall of Ford's friendship with Conrad. Ford and his wife, Elsie, had been having troubles for some time, and each seems to have tried to draw the Conrads into their conflict. That, coupled with Ford's ability to irritate and alienate many of their mutual friends and acquaintances, finally resulted in a break in their friendship that was never fully repaired.

Despite some progress on *Under Western Eyes*, much of 1909 seems to have been taken up with Conrad's struggles with health and financial issues as well as writer's block. His only completed work was an essay entitled "The Silence of the Sea," which was published in September. In late November, Conrad began writing "The Secret Sharer," usually considered to be one of his finest stories. He wrote with considerable speed, and, for one of the few times in his writing career, seemed genuinely pleased with the result. Progress on *Under Western Eyes* continued to be difficult, but Conrad worked hard to finish the novel, finally completing it in January 1910. No other novel would be such a trial for him. Suffering through periods of writer's block, financial straits, and physical and emotional illness, Conrad wrote the novel that was closer to him than any of his other works, a novel in which he would grapple with problems of betrayal, revolutionary politics, and Russian autocracy. All of these issues were close to Conrad's personal experience, and spending so much of his life immersed in that world of intrigue must have been like reliving some of his childhood experiences. The end result was that he suffered a complete breakdown that lasted some months. Conrad's breakdown may have resulted in more than just physical and emotional illness. Many commentators see *Under Western Eyes* as the high-water mark of Conrad's artistic creativity, arguing that, except for *The Shadow-Line*, almost all of what Conrad wrote afterwards was artistically inferior.

After his recovery, Conrad turned to "A Smile of Fortune," which was a return to his sea fiction. In June, the Conrad family moved to Capel House in Orlestone, a much more quiet area, and exactly what Conrad needed at the time. In July, he wrote three essays for the *Daily Mail* ("A Happy Wanderer," "The Ascending Effort," and "The Life Beyond"), which were later included in *Notes on Life and Letters*. In August, Conrad's work received recognition in the form of a permanent government grant of £100 per year, and in September he finished "A Smile of Fortune" and planned to work on other stories. Around the same time, he completed "Prince Roman" and then began "The Partner" in October and "Freya of the Seven Isles" in December. Both stories were completed in March of 1911. In May, Conrad made a more concerted effort on *Chance* and finally broke through his writer's block. In fact, he made considerable progress once he returned to the novel. Another important literary friendship began in July, when Conrad met André Gide, who would become a life-long friend. During the summer, Conrad also worked on *A Personal Record*, and the book version of *Under Western Eyes* appeared in October of 1911. Reviews were generally positive but often misunderstood the novel, and once again sales were modest. Although Conrad remained more popular with the critics than with the reading public, the groundwork for a change was beginning, as his following in America and France was growing.

In late 1911, Conrad was making steady progress on *Chance* and supplemented his income by selling some manuscripts to an American collector,

John Quinn, with whom he would become friends. *A Personal Record* was published in January of 1912 to generally favorable reviews. *Chance* began to be serialized in January of 1912, and Conrad finished the novel in late March 1912. About this time, he also wrote two articles for *The English Review* on the *Titanic* disaster, a subject close to his heart because of his background as a sailor and also because the manuscript of "Karain," which he had sold to Quinn, went down with the ship. In May, Conrad began work on what would become *Victory* and continued to work on it steadily through the summer and fall of 1912.

October 1912 seems to mark the beginning of a change in Conrad's career. His collection of stories *'Twixt Land and Sea*, which contained "The Secret Sharer," "A Smile of Fortune," and "Freya of the Seven Isles," was published and sold better than any of Conrad's previous books. The collection was also well received by the critics. Most commentators point to the publication of *Chance* as the beginning of Conrad's financial success, and it certainly is, but *'Twixt Land and Sea* was a clear precursor, and so between the publication of *'Twixt Land and Sea* and the money from the manuscripts he sold to Quinn, Conrad's financial situation was finally beginning to look up.

While continuing to work on *Victory*, Conrad wrote "The Inn of the Two Witches" in late 1912, and the first part of 1913 was spent in working on *Victory* and preparing the book version of *Chance*. In the summer of 1913, Conrad made another intellectual friend in Bertrand Russell, who admired Conrad's works, and the rest of 1913 was spent largely on *Victory*. In November, Conrad started "The Planter of Malata," which he finished in December, and shortly thereafter he wrote "Because of the Dollars," which was originally conceived of as part of *Victory*. The January 1914 publication of *Chance* in book form marked the true turning point in Conrad's financial circumstances and popularity. The novel was fairly well reviewed, but there were reservations. Henry James was one of the first to seriously criticize the novel when he suggested that Conrad had prioritized form over content. Meanwhile, *Victory* continued to grow, and Conrad finally finished it in mid-1914.

In the spring of 1914, Conrad's friend, Józef Retinger, a Pole living in England, invited Conrad and his family to take a vacation in Poland. It was now more than twenty years since he had seen his homeland and Conrad quickly warmed to the idea. World War I broke out shortly after Conrad arrived in Poland, however, and the trip turned out to be rather dangerous. Because of Conrad's British citizenship, he could have been imprisoned once Austria and England declared war, but his Polish background and the fact that he stayed in a relatively isolated region helped to keep him out of trouble. Nevertheless, returning to England was by no means easy. Conrad's bouts of gout and Jessie's nagging knee injury made travel difficult. Furthermore, in order for them to return to England, they had to travel through hostile territories. After making their arrangements, the Conrads began their return journey in early October, traveling first to Vienna and then on to Italy. Finally, finding sea passage from Genoa, they arrived in England in November. The journey was both mentally and physically fatiguing and left Conrad ill upon arriving.

In early 1915, Conrad had been talking about taking up the long-neglected *The Rescue*, but it would yet be some time before he would complete it. At the same time, he began work on a short novel, *The Shadow-Line*, which he had planned a number of years earlier and which many commentators feel to be Conrad's finest work written after *Under Western Eyes*. In February 1916, Conrad's collection of short stories, *Within the Tides*, was published and included "The Planter of Malata," "The Partner," "The Inn of the Two Witches," and "Because of the Dollars." It is often considered Conrad's weakest collection. Nevertheless, the book was well received and sold well. Clearly, Conrad's reputation was now such that his books could expect good reviews and good sales. *Victory* was published in book form in March and following on the heels of *Chance*'s success, its sales were also strong. Today, the novel has many supporters and also an equal number of detractors, but when it was first published the book's detractors were few.

Meanwhile, Conrad finished *The Shadow-Line* in mid-December, a novel based in part upon Conrad's own experience in obtaining his first command and a story of that imperceptible movement from youth to adulthood. Conrad's writing in the early part of 1916 proceeded even more slowly than it had the previous year with only "The Warrior's Soul" to show for his efforts. Later that year, Conrad met Jane Anderson, a young and attractive woman who would become the object of speculation by some biographers as to whether she and Conrad had an affair. It is impossible to know for certain, but they were certainly mutually attracted.

All this time, World War I was raging. Conrad's stance toward the war was ambivalent; having seen too much of life and being too skeptical, he certainly could not get caught up in jingoism. At the same time, though, he felt loyal to his homeland and to his adopted country, both of whom were significantly affected by the war. Conrad's actual activities surrounding the war effort were limited to some maritime war maneuvers. In the fall of 1916, he served as a kind of guest observer of naval activities, visiting shipyards, watching target practice, and taking short voyages off the coast of England, as well as going up for a short flight in a reconnaissance plane. His short story "The Tale" seems to have resulted from those activities. In addition, Conrad wrote two essays related to his experiences: "Flight" and "The Unlighted Coast." "Flight" was later to appear in *Notes on Life and Letters*. Like so many others at home, Conrad did not remain untouched by the tragedy of the war. In early 1917, Conrad's friend the poet Edward Thomas was killed, and some time later Borys suffered shell shock after being gassed. In March of 1917, *The Shadow-Line* appeared in book form and was dedicated to Borys and the other young men who were becoming adults while fighting the war. The book was again well received and solidified Conrad's position as one of the most important authors of his time. In July, Conrad appears to have begun working on a novel that he had been thinking about for some time: *The Arrow of Gold*. Apart from this he wrote only a few short pieces during all of 1917, prefaces to new editions of some of his works, as well as one for Garnett's book on Turgenev.

In November, Jessie's knee condition became bad enough to require further medical attention, and the family moved to London for her treatment. During that time, Conrad had the chance to meet with many friends, something he had missed at Capel House. Despite Conrad's increased social life, work progressed fairly quickly on *The Arrow of Gold*. Returning to Capel House in February, Conrad continued working on *The Arrow of Gold*, making good progress and completing the novel before they had to return to London again in June for more treatment on Jessie's knee. Shortly after finishing the novel, Conrad wrote two more essays: "Well Done" and "First News," both of which later appeared in *Notes on Life and Letters*. Around this time, Conrad once again turned his attention to *The Rescue*. Having returned to Capel House in August, he spent the fall of 1918 working on *The Rescue*, but in December he took time out to write "The Crime of Partition," which was also later published in *Notes on Life and Letters*. This essay, along with others like it, shows an increased interest in political issues, particularly those regarding Poland.

In early 1919, plans for a collected edition of Conrad's works began to move forward, and Conrad started writing a series of "Author's Notes." In February, he also began to work in earnest once again on *The Rescue*. In March, work on the novel was briefly interrupted when the Conrads were forced to move to another house, Spring Grove. Meanwhile, *The Rescue* sprawled, and work was again interrupted by illness and, briefly, by work on another essay entitled "Confidence" (also published in *Notes on Life and Letters*). After some twenty-three years, Conrad finally completed *The Rescue* at the end of May, and that summer was spent revising it for book publication and writing more "Author's Notes" for the collected edition. Another important development occurred that summer when Conrad sold the film rights to his works for £3,080. This piece of good fortune, along with the good sales of *The Arrow of Gold*, and similar expectations for *The Rescue*, put Conrad in a very good financial situation. Certainly, since the publication of *Chance*, Conrad's finances had much improved, but increased expenditure followed increased income, as he still tended to spend beyond his means.

The critical reception for *The Arrow of Gold* was not nearly as positive as it had been for Conrad's other books, and most later commentators have concurred. Conrad's letters of this time often reveal a tone of weariness and the feeling that his abilities were past their prime. Later that year, the Conrads decided to move yet again, this time to Oswalds in Bishopsbourne. For several months, Conrad seems to have done little if any writing. In November 1919, Conrad again took up a stage adaptation, this time of *The Secret Agent*. Late that same month, the Conrads traveled to Liverpool for yet another operation on Jessie's knee. It was hoped that the procedure would be successful, but further operations were necessary before her condition improved significantly. Over the next few months, Conrad continued to work on the adaptation of *The Secret Agent*, finishing in March of 1920. Conrad also continued to write more "Author's Notes" for the collected edition. Around this time, *The Rescue* appeared as a book, and its reception was much better than that of *The Arrow of Gold*, a notable exception, though, being Virginia Woolf's review.

In June, Conrad began work on his next novel; then tentatively titled *The Isle of Rest*, the novel would later become *Suspense*. The book progressed slowly through the summer, and in September Conrad and Pinker collaborated on a film script version of "Gaspar Ruiz," finishing it in October. The manuscript is no longer extant, and it was never filmed. That same month, Conrad wrote the last "Author's Note" for the collected edition, and in November he adapted another of his stories, "Because of the Dollars," for the theatre, but the work (*Laughing Anne*) was not staged. All this time, Conrad made little progress on *Suspense* and once more he fell ill.

In early 1921, *Notes on Life and Letters* was published, and making slow progress on *Suspense*, Conrad next attempted something he had never tried before: he translated Bruno Winawer's play *The Book of Job* from Polish into English. However, the play was never staged. About this time, Conrad also wrote an essay, "The Dover Patrol," for *The Times*. In the fall, unable to make headway on *Suspense*, Conrad laid it aside and began *The Rover*, but this project, too, progressed slowly. *The Rover* was conceived of as a story, but as had happened so often in the past, it grew into a novel. A great blow to Conrad occurred in February 1922 when J. B. Pinker, Conrad's agent and long-time friend, died. Pinker had been patient with Conrad's numerous delays and requests for money, and although there was occasional friction between them, Pinker was a loyal supporter and generous friend to Conrad, and Conrad felt a great loss at Pinker's death.

In April, work on *The Rover* picked up, and the novel was essentially finished in June. In November, the stage version of *The Secret Agent* was performed but was poorly reviewed and poorly attended. Later that month, Conrad wrote an essay "Outside Literature," the only writing he had done for some time. By this time in his life, Conrad was expressing a great deal of fatigue, and this feeling was directly related to his inability to write. In January of 1923, though, Conrad began working again in earnest on *Suspense* and continued fairly steadily through March, only taking time out to write an introduction for Thomas Beer's biography of Crane, along with a preface to a new edition of Crane's *The Red Badge of Courage.*

Having earlier been convinced by Doubleday to come to America to speak and promote his books, Conrad left for New York in April. Arriving in early May, Conrad remained in America a month, amidst a whirlwind series of readings, interviews, meetings, and public adulation. After returning to England in June, Conrad spent time recovering from the experience. In July, he wrote an essay "Christmas Day at Sea" and began work again on *Suspense* – but with little result. In August, Conrad wrote another essay: "The *Torrens* – A Personal Tribute," and did not do any significant work again until November, when he wrote one of his most important non-fiction pieces: "Geography and Some Explorers." In December, *The Rover* was published, and although it sold well, it was not popular with the critics.

In early 1924, Conrad still hoped to complete *Suspense*, but he made little if any progress. In April, he wrote a preface to a collection of his stories entitled *Shorter Tales.* Also in April, Ford talked Conrad into publishing their collaborative tale *The Nature of the Crime* in book form, and Conrad agreed to write a preface for it, which he completed in May. About this time, Ramsay MacDonald offered Conrad knighthood, but he declined. Shortly afterwards, Conrad began an essay entitled "Legends." He made little headway, and it would prove to be Conrad's last work. On August 2 1924, Conrad experienced chest pain and shortness of breath. Doctors came and thought that his condition was not serious. He seemed better the next morning, but about 8.30 am he fell from his chair with a cry and died. He was laid to rest on August 7 in Canterbury.

Chapter 2

Conrad's context

Wars, political uprisings, colonial rule and unrest, and the ebb and flow of economic fortunes all play a part in the literature of the late nineteenth and early twentieth centuries. Important cultural issues, such as woman's rights, increased industrialism and mechanization, scientific and technological advances, and the changing political climate were equally influential. Furthermore, the literary, philosophical, and artistic movements of this period directly relate to the literature that appeared. This chapter will outline these contexts and show how Conrad's works both influenced and were influenced by them.

History and politics

Even more than most British novelists, Conrad was affected not only by important historical events in England but also by those on the continent. Given his years in Poland, France, Russia and the Orient, Conrad's experience was far more cosmopolitan than that of most of his fellow novelists in England. In particular, Conrad was significantly influenced by events affecting France, Poland, and Russia during the nineteenth and early part of the twentieth centuries. These events would form the context for Conrad's life and also for much of his fiction.

In the case of France, the influence on Conrad appears in the setting for several of his works and in their effect on Poland's political situation. From the time of his youth, Conrad was especially interested in Napoleonic France. Emerging from the turmoil of the French revolution of 1789, Napoleon Bonaparte came to power shortly after the Brumaire coup of November 1799. Within a few years, he solidified his power and became absolute ruler. Napoleon began his campaigns against France's neighbors, first invading northern Italy and defeating Austria in the Battle of Marengo. In 1802, he negotiated the Treaty of Amiens with England, but the treaty was short-lived, as both sides failed to abide by its terms, and by 1804 France and England were at war again. Although defeated at sea in the Battle of Trafalgar in October of 1805, Napoleon countered with a decisive victory a month later against the Austrians (allies of England) in the Battle of Austerlitz. The following year, France defeated Prussia in the Battle of Jena and the Battle of Auerstadt and then took on the Russian army in February of 1807, first in the Battle of Eylau, which resulted in a draw, and then in June in the Battle of Friedland, which resulted in a French victory and a treaty with Russia. For the next several years, Napoleon consolidated his power and annexed a number of territories, while the war with England took a turn in which both sides tried to exert economic pressure on the other. In 1812, Napoleon embarked on his disastrous Russian campaign. Although he had defeated the Russians in the Battle of Friedland, invading Russia was a different matter entirely. Practicing a scorched earth policy of retreat, the Russian army deprived the French of the ability to resupply along the way, and although the French army occupied Moscow in October of 1812, they had little to show for it except enormous losses. The famous ensuing retreat in the midst of the brutal Russian winter cost Napoleon most of what remained of the nearly 600,000 troops who had begun the offensive. Both "The Duel" and "The Warrior's Soul" chronicle the hardships of the retreating French forces. The failed Russian campaign was the beginning of the end for Napoleon, who was later defeated in the Battle of Leipzig in October of 1813 and finally beaten once and for all at the Battle of Waterloo in June of 1815.

Suspense was to have been Conrad's definitive fictional statement on Napoleonic France, perhaps in some ways the European equivalent of *Nostromo*, but age, illness, and fatigue rendered the unfinished novel only a fraction of Conrad's vision of it. Along with *Suspense, The Rover,* "The Duel," and "The Warrior's Soul" would use the fertile soil of Napoleonic France as the basis for investigating the nature of the relationship between the individual and larger political forces.

While France, particularly Napoleonic France, served primarily as a setting and political backdrop for Conrad's writings, Russia had a more immediate impact on Conrad's life and work. With the notable exception of *Under Western Eyes,* Conrad did not use Russia as a setting for his works. Nineteenth-century Russian history and politics, however, had a great deal of influence on Conrad, in particular, Russia's interaction with Poland and Russia's revolutionary politics.

After the defeat of the French army under Napoleon, Russia became the pre-eminent power on land for some forty years. Nicholas I, Tsar during most of this time, was a strong defender of monarchial rule in the midst of widespread democratic movements throughout Europe. With Nicholas's staunch defense of autocracy came an increasingly corrupt and entrenched bureaucracy that expanded its role into all aspects of society and came to symbolize the increasing distance between the people and the government, as this bureaucracy became almost a machine-like entity, independent of the people who ran it. Russia's defeat in the Crimean War of 1853–6, however, changed its position of power. Shortly before the end of the war, Alexander II assumed the throne and began a series of changes with the purpose of modernizing Russia, which he felt had become backward, resulting in Russia's defeat. The two most prominent changes were the abolition of serfdom and the reformation of the judicial system. Other lesser reforms followed. Despite these reforms, political unrest continued, with many people demanding liberties akin to those enjoyed in the West. With government resistance to such changes came increased revolutionary activity. In 1876, the Land and Freedom party was formed, some of whose members favored terrorist tactics to gain their ends. The People's Will wing of the Land and Freedom party split off in 1879, with the specific idea of pursuing revolutionary force, and in 1881 they succeeded in assassinating Alexander II. In 1891, a famine resulting from poor crop-yield rejuvenated revolutionary activities, which continued until the fall of the monarchy in 1917. Political upheaval marked this period and resulted in numerous political assassinations, including the assassination in 1904 of Vyacheslav Konstantinovich Plehve, Minister of the Interior. This incident (as did the assassination of Alexander II) would serve as the basis for Victor Haldin's assassination of Mr. de P— in *Under Western Eyes*.

Russia's rule of Poland would be of particular and immediate effect on Conrad's life and works, but Russian autocracy, bureaucracy, and revolutionary politics would also be an important influence. In addition to *Under Western Eyes*, several of Conrad's other works consider the idea of revolutionary politics and the governments they opposed, all modeled after the revolutionary politics of the nineteenth and early twentieth centuries. The most prominent of these revolutionary camps were the Anarchists and the Socialists. In Conrad's works, all of his revolutionaries (except those in *Nostromo* and "Gaspar Ruiz") are either Anarchists or Socialists.

Although Anarchism's origins can be traced to earlier sources, it is largely a phenomenon of the nineteenth and early twentieth centuries and largely associated with the revolutionary politics of France, Italy, and Russia. Pierre-Joseph Proudhon is often considered the founder of nineteenth-century Anarchist thought. In such works as *What is Property?* (1840), Proudhon considers the basic ideas that permeate Anarchist philosophy: that social problems result from private property and political power. In particular, Anarchists rejected the concept of a centralized state and instead argued for much smaller regional forms of governance. Proudhon influenced a number of other political thinkers, one the most important of whom was Mikhail Bakunin, who had been exiled from Russia because of his revolutionary activities. One of the significant differences between Proudhon and Bakunin, however, was their methodology. While Proudhon advocated a gradualist and peaceful transition to a stateless, propertyless society, Bakunin advocated any approach by which he could bring about such a change, particularly favoring the violent overthrow of governments. In the end, Bakunin was the more influential of the two, and his methods later became a common tool for many Anarchists. Although various strains of Anarchism existed, Bakunin's violent revolution was perhaps the most influential and resulted in numerous political assassinations in the latter part of the nineteenth century.

Anarchism and Socialism had some important similarities, particularly in their view of capitalist economics and the issue of property. Nevertheless, significant differences existed as well, and in the 1870s a major split arose. Despite their differences, however, various revolutionary wings of the Socialist movement advocated methods akin to those of the violent wings of the Anarchist movement, and the political assassinations carried out, particularly by the Russian Socialists, were remarkably similar to those carried out by their Anarchist counterparts. Like Anarchism, Socialism had its origins in earlier thought, and, also like Anarchism, it is essentially a nineteenth- and twentieth-century phenomenon. Again, as with Anarchism, one can point to the rise of capitalist economics and the industrial revolution as primary causes for its emergence. The primary points upon which the Anarchists and Socialists diverge lie in the role of government and the role of private property. Anarchists rejected strong, centralized government and the concept of private property. In contrast, some Socialist groups proposed a strong, centralized government and limited private property. Even so, distinguishing between the main tenets of Anarchism and those of Socialism is not always easy. Some Socialist camps urged for complete nationalization of property and industry, while others advocated a more selective approach. Similarly, some Socialist camps advocated a strong central government, while others urged for a more disperse form of government.

Several figures have been credited with the origins of Socialist thought in the nineteenth century. In France, for example, Henri de Saint-Simon and François-Marie-Charles Fourier argued for early Socialist ideas. Saint-Simon saw the capitalist economic system as fostering an extreme individualism that he believed would eventually destroy the social order, while Fourier felt that the competition inherent in capitalist economics was its primary drawback.

Other early French Socialists include Étienne Cabet, Louis Blanc, Louis-Auguste Blanqui, and Proudhon. (Proudhon's inclusion here emphasizes the common origins of Anarchism and Socialism.) Of these early Socialists, Blanqui was the closest to the revolutionaries who appear in Conrad's works and is noted more for his revolutionary activities than for his revolutionary thought. Despite the contributions of these and other individuals, Socialism is linked primarily to the ideas of Karl Marx and Friedrich Engels. Their *Communist Manifesto* (1848) appeared in the same year as the general democratic uprising that spread across much of Europe. Citing both the capitalist and the class systems as the causes of social problems, they advocated a classless society in which workers rather than industrialists would be rewarded for their labor.

Socialist thought in the nineteenth century engendered a variety of important movements. One of the more significant was the populist movement in Russia. Lead by Alexandr Herzen, the populists looked to the peasant communities as a model for a Socialist society and hoped to foster a widespread peasant revolt in order to bring about social change. While many of Herzen's followers argued for a peaceful, evolutionary approach to social change, focusing on educating the population and disseminating political propaganda, others lost faith in the possibility of a peasant uprising and broke away, urging direct terrorist attacks instead. In this more radical Socialism, the lines between Anarchism and Socialism blur considerably. It was these radical Socialists, along with other Socialists with similar ideas, such as the Socialist Revolutionary Party, who were responsible for most of the assassinations and terrorist activities that occurred in Russia at the time.

Conrad used the revolutionary politics of this period as important raw material for a number of his works. Thus, revolutionaries and Anarchists appear prominently in *The Secret Agent*, *Under Western Eyes*, "The Informer," and "The Anarchist." And although *Nostromo* and "Gaspar Ruiz" are set in South America, their revolutionary politics differ little from those in Conrad's European political works.

Even more than French and Russian history and politics, the influence of Poland's history and politics was paramount to Conrad's development as a writer. Although Conrad wrote little that directly relates to Poland, the events that impinged on Poland's fate during the nineteenth and early twentieth centuries affected Conrad both directly and indirectly, and they consistently and subtly make their way into all of his best works.

After the third partition in 1795, Poland did not exist as an independent entity for 123 years but was divided among Prussia, Austria, and Russia. With a long cultural tradition, Poles remained strongly nationalistic and periodically revolted against foreign control, particularly Russian control. The two most prominent revolts occurred in 1830 and 1863. Beginning in Warsaw in November, the revolt of 1830 soon became widespread and was not finally put down until September of 1831. Harsh reprisals followed, and Russian rule became even more restrictive. One of those involved in the revolt was Prince Roman Sanguszko, whom Conrad claims to have met as a boy and whose experience Conrad would fictionalize in "Prince Roman."

Conrad's family and relatives lived primarily in Russian controlled Poland. Beginning around 1861, conflicts arose between the Polish people and their Russian rulers. Demonstrators in Warsaw fought with Russian troops, with some of the demonstrators dying in the conflict. Afterwards, seeking to control the Poles, the Russians appointed Aleksander Wielopolski to head the Polish government. Wielopolski, though, was enormously unpopular, and the Whites (the more moderate opposition) and the Reds (the more radical opposition) both began underground operations against Wielopolski's government and against Russian rule. These operations erupted into a full-scale uprising in January of 1863. The Russians eventually put down the uprising in the fall of 1864, capturing and executing the leader of the Reds, Romuald Traugutt. In the years after the revolt, the Poles once again experienced strong reprisals. Many were executed or exiled, had their lands confiscated, or suffered other repressive measures.

The results of the 1863 uprising were particularly disastrous for Conrad. His father's political activism led to the family's exile and the eventual death of Conrad's parents. Other relatives were either killed or imprisoned. These events, as well as the repressive measures implemented in the aftermath of the rebellion, affected Conrad's view of Russia and also colored his view of revolution, revolutionaries, and politics in general. Throughout his life, Conrad remained suspicious of all political activity, and his dark, skeptical outlook on the world can be traced to his early experiences in Poland and Russia.

In addition to the consequences of the 1863 uprising, the convoluted political alliances in Europe left Poland with little hope of help from sympathetic neighbors, such as France and England. Because of concern over Prussian and Austrian strength, France and England strengthened ties with Russia. Consequently, with Russia as a political adversary to Prussia and Austria, and countries such as France and England acting as allies to Russia and opponents of Prussia and Austria, Poland was in effect caught between these larger political struggles. Although France and England may have been perfectly content to condemn Austrian and Prussian control of Polish territories, they could not do so without tacitly condemning Russian control of

Polish lands as well. This complex political climate also contributed to Conrad's pessimistic outlook for Poland's future, since it looked as if Poland would be forever caught between powerful opposing forces.

Poland's fate in some ways resembled and was indirectly affected by another phenomenon occurring about this time: the new imperialism. From about 1875 until the beginning of World War I, Western countries engaged in an unprecedented race to divide up the non-Western world. Colonial activities had been ongoing since about 1500 – but never with such speed, competition, and insatiability. In addition to such traditional colonial powers as Spain, England, France, the Netherlands, and Portugal, new Western nations entered the fray, such as Italy, Belgium, Germany, the United States, and others began acquiring colonial territories. By the beginning of World War I, approximately 85 per cent of the world was under Western control. The result was that tensions among competing nations increased and further complicated the already complex political climate in Europe.

Poland was indirectly affected by these activities since the competing colonial powers were also among those who controlled Polish territories or who were either allied with or against those powers. In a more symbolic way, though, the new imperialism related to the Polish question in that, like the conquered peoples of European colonies, the Poles had seen competing European nations divide and conquer their territory. Thus, criticism of Poland's situation became more difficult because of widespread support for essentially the same practice elsewhere. Conrad found himself right in the middle of all of this activity. Since he had begun his maritime career in the 1870s and spent most of it in the service of colonial endeavors in one capacity or another, he was greatly influenced by the effect that the new imperialism had on Poland's fate. Much of his time was spent in Southeast Asia, experiencing first hand the role of the conquering European nations in the non-European world. Furthermore, Conrad's briefer experiences in Africa and South America should not be discounted, in that they both affected him and resulted in no fewer than five literary works. The majority of Conrad's fictional writings are set in the colonial world, and, had Conrad not been part of that world, his fiction would have been drastically different. Conrad's experience also allowed him to look at colonialism much more objectively than could many of his contemporaries. Along with his first-hand experience in the non-Western world, Conrad had other unique perspectives that allowed him to look at the colonial process differently from his contemporaries. His own background was not unlike that of the colonized peoples he encountered. Conrad was a Russian subject and grew up in an occupied country, and although his experience under Russian rule was different in many ways from that of non-European colonial subjects, it was also similar in many ways. This unique background allowed him to see colonialism through the eyes of both the colonizers and the colonized.

The end of the new imperialism coincided with the outbreak of World War I, an event which would have a direct impact on Conrad and on Poland's fate, which had begun to occupy more of Conrad's efforts than it ever had before. Although Poland's dilemma was always in the background of Conrad's works, after 1914 he took direct steps to address the situation. With the victory of the Russian Revolution and the defeat of Austria and Germany in the war in 1918, a new Polish state emerged from the wreckage of World War I. During the war, Conrad wrote three essays concerning the Polish situation and actively lobbied on behalf of Polish independence.

In addition to the war's direct affect on Conrad through his interest in Polish independence, he was personally affected by it through the death or injury of those he knew. Unlike many of his fellow writers, Conrad did not experience a profound disillusionment as a result of the war – primarily because his disillusionment had solidified long beforehand. As a consequence of his experiences as a child and as a young man, Conrad had long held a profoundly skeptical view of the inviolability of civilization and the perfectibility of humanity. Nevertheless, World War I did reinforce Conrad's already dark view of the world.

Although Modernist literature is often characterized as being relatively isolated from political, historical, and cultural events and as focusing instead on the individual, Conrad's works run an important middle course, as he consistently focuses on the individual – but always in the midst of political, historical, and cultural forces.

Cultural issues

Since the late eighteenth century, England had been moving increasingly rapidly away from an agrarian economy and toward an industrial economy. By 1850, half of England's population resided in cities, and a large percentage was associated with industry. Within a few years, large industrial cities appeared throughout England and, despite the resulting prosperity, wealth remained in the hands of a few. The industrial revolution brought with it numerous problems, such as poor infrastructure, housing, sanitation, and transportation, as well as extensive environmental pollution. It also brought poor working conditions, low wages, and long working days. Safe working conditions were not seen as a priority, and thus serious injuries were not uncommon. With unionization strongly discouraged, workers had few rights, and because of a surplus of cheap labor, they had little choice but to accept whatever terms employers offered. Conrad did not write novels of social conscience. Nevertheless, born in 1857, he lived through more of the rise of the industrial age than did most of his contemporaries. More important for Conrad's works, though, was the side effect of industrialization, that is the profound increase in the role of technology in society and in the work place. With this increased role came increased mechanization, alienation, and de-humanization. The isolation of the individual in the modern world was a favorite topic of Conrad, and his characters often depict one as ultimately alone in the world.

Along with England's increased industrialism and mechanization, women's inequality was a prominent issue of the time. Concerns such as women's property rights, women in the workplace, and women's suffrage were hotly debated. During the nineteenth century, women gained various victories in their struggle for equality, but change was slow. The issue of women in the workplace was a crucial aspect of the woman question, and there were two parts to this problem. The first was that ideally a woman was supposed to marry and become a selfless caregiver to her children and husband. She should work only if she could not marry and had no other alternative. Unmarried women whose families were not wealthy, however, found them-selves in a precarious position. For working-class women, employment options were limited to becoming servants or factory workers. For middle-class women, the options were even more limited: they could become gov-ernesses, schoolteachers, or companions. Later in the nineteenth century, middle-class women could sometimes do secretarial work or perform certain factory jobs. At no point, though, could they compete with men for clerk positions or other more prestigious and better-paid occupations.

Conrad brings into his fiction the question of a woman's place in society in various ways. In "Heart of Darkness," for instance, the women are "out of it." They inhabit a place in society away from the harsh realities of the man's world. This resembles the traditional nineteenth-century view of women occupying and providing a sanctified home, removed from the corrupting influence of the world of men. On a more general level, issues of women's rights appear in *Chance*, for instance, in which Conrad's narrator, Marlow, presents Mrs. Fyne as a staunch feminist and clearly disapproves of her views, while at the same time showing that Flora de Barral's plight results largely because she is a woman. Similarly, in *The Secret Agent*, Winnie marries Verloc solely for the security he represents because, as a woman, she has no other viable employment options. The issue of women also enters Conrad's writing in his audience. From the outset, commentators have considered Conrad to be a man's author and have seen his reading public as consisting primarily of men. Recently, some critics have suggested otherwise and argued that in fact Conrad always considered women to be part of his primary audience. Much of the evidence for this view has to do with the fact that much of the reading public consisted of women. Furthermore, Conrad's works of his later career in particular, with their prominent elements of love and romance, were clearly directed at a female reading public.

Perhaps the single most important cultural issue of the latter part of the nineteenth century, though, was the nature of Western civilization itself. Europeans had long held that their view of the world was pre-eminent, a world view based upon transcendent truths and sanctioned by God. The nineteenth century, however, saw this idea come into question, and throughout the century, traditionally held truths came under scrutiny. At that time, the Western world view would be challenged seemingly on all fronts and at breakneck speed. In the 1820s, Charles Lyell began observing geological formations and wondering about what he saw. The standard view, based on theological teachings, was that the earth was roughly 4,000 years old. What Lyell saw, however, caused him to question such a figure. His *Principles of Geology* (1830–3) would become a revolutionary work in geology and in scientific inquiry in general, resulting in a reassessment of the earth's age. The work of Charles Darwin would prove even more revolutionary. In the 1830s, Darwin took a voyage aboard *The Beagle* on a mission of scientific discovery. He stopped at the Galapagos Islands off the coast of South America, and in this geographically isolated region, he noted interesting variations among the animal life there. The result of these discoveries eventually grew into his theory of natural selection, in which he posited that individuals within a species compete with one another for shelter, food, breeding opportunities, etc. and that consequently those individuals best able to compete are those most likely to survive and pass on their traits to their offspring. It would be over twenty years after his return from the Galapagos Islands, though, before Darwin would publish his findings in his landmark work *The Origin of Species* (1859). Darwin's theory, of course, challenged commonly held ideas regarding the origin of the earth and of human beings. Beginning with the famous confrontation between T. H. Huxley and Bishop Samuel Wilberforce, this issue would be debated and would become one of the more significant challenges to contemporary thinking about the nature of the universe.

Challenges to traditional views of the world arose not only in the field of science. Various other fields of intellectual study also presented challenges to such thinking. Alternatives to capitalist economics as well as to class structure and centralized systems of government presented challenges to the way Europeans had usually conceived society to exist. Furthermore, the discovery of such phenomena as non-Euclidian geometry and relativist physics argued for the indeterminacy of things – a stark contrast to the traditionally held view of a world of transcendent truths and certainty. Finally, increased contact with the non-Western world through the opening of Japan in 1854 and the new imperialism brought Westerners into greater contact with non-Western society, philosophy, culture, and art. And for some, such contact provided viable alternatives to traditional Western culture and society.

For generations, most Westerners had viewed their way of looking at the world as the only one possible, a view evolving out of Christian theology and ultimately based upon absolute truths. Consequently, they saw Western culture's advanced technology and civilization as validating their world view, with all other ways of looking at the world appearing inferior, backward, and wrong. However, the challenges to such Western views that appeared in the nineteenth century brought into question fundamental assumptions about the nature of the world and the nature of the universe. In this way, the moorings of Western civilization began to erode, and the very idea of absolute truths came under scrutiny. The effects of this cultural climate profoundly influenced the world in which Conrad wrote.

Philosophical milieu

The major philosophical debate that would have a direct affect on Conrad's writing was Positivism and the various responses to it. Conrad also seems to have been familiar with the works of Arthur Schopenhauer, and his ideas appear to have influenced Conrad's thinking.

During the nineteenth century, scientific activity and discovery exploded exponentially. Science made perhaps more progress during this century than it had during the previous twenty centuries combined, including some of the most important scientific discoveries ever made: Michael Faraday's work in field theory; Hermann von Helmholtz's, Julius Robert Von Mayer's, and James Prescott Joule's work on the conservation of energy; Lyell's work in geology; Darwin's work in biological evolution; Augustin-Jean Fresnel's work with light theory; James Clerk Maxwell's and William Thompson's work in electricity and magnetism; John Dalton's theory of atoms; Theodor Schwann's and Matthias Schleiden's cell theory; Louis Pasteur's and Robert Koch's work with germ theory; along with the work of numerous others all occurred during or shortly before the nineteenth century. These discoveries resulted not only in greater scientific knowledge, but also in greater prestige. Consequently, for many, science had achieved a place that had previously been reserved only for religion, and people gained unprecedented confidence in science's ability to provide certainty.

One result of these scientific discoveries was that many traditionally held truths came under scrutiny, another was science's influence on the philosophy of the time. Through the work of Jeremy Bentham, Auguste Comte, John Stuart Mill, and those who followed them, such as Herbert Spencer, Cesare Lombroso, Hippolyte Taine, Ernest Renan, G. H. Lewes, Emile Durkheim, Leslie Stephen, and many others, the increased prestige of science and the increased confidence people placed in it resulted in Scientific Positivism, a school of thought that proceeded upon the premise that all knowledge could be determined by employing the scientific method. As a result, many disciplines adopted scientific methodology as their primary means of inquiry. Nor were the arts immune from this influence: Realism and Naturalism were direct products of the rise of science, their primary assumptions and techniques being basically scientific in nature.

Not all thinkers accepted the Positivist model. As early as Søren Kierkegaard and as late as the early twentieth century and beyond, a number of thinkers questioned Positivism. Wilhelm Dilthey, Edmund Husserl, Friedrich Nietzsche, Henri Bergson, and others questioned the wisdom of employing a scientific model to explain all phenomena, even human beings and human social activity. Like these contemporaries, Conrad felt that any system that sought to explain all phenomena was suspect, and although he respected science he rejected the all-encompassing Positivist model. For example, in *Victory*, *Lord Jim*, *The Secret Agent*, "Heart of Darkness," and elsewhere Conrad questions the ability of science and facts to provide certainty. In *Victory*, Heyst comes to realize that human relationships not facts provide fulfillment in life. In *Lord Jim*, Marlow feels that only through understanding a fact's subjective context is knowledge perhaps possible. Conrad's questioning of Scientific Positivism is even more clear in "Heart of Darkness" and *The Secret Agent*. In "Heart of Darkness," Marlow presents the Belgian doctor who measures the heads of his patients as a fool, and in *The Secret Agent*, Conrad ridicules Positivism when Comrade Ossipon draws conclusions about Winnie Verloc's psychology based upon her facial features.

In addition to Scientific Positivism, Conrad was familiar with and influenced by the philosophy of Arthur Schopenhauer. Schopenhauer's primary contribution to the history of philosophy is his *The World as Will and Representation* (1818). Influenced by Immanuel Kant, particularly Kant's ideas of noumena and phenomena, Schopenhauer argued that the physical world with which human beings interact is merely a representation of reality and not reality itself. He refers to Will as the reality that human beings cannot apprehend as phenomena. Largely, this Will is the will to be, the desire to exist. Will, however, can never be fully satisfied except through its no longer desiring what makes it what it is, in other words, by no longer desiring to exist; hence, the Will can only lead to despair because it desires to be something it cannot be, that is a desire to exist that does not desire to exist, and furthermore because for much of the phenomenal world the Will to exist can only be at the expense of others' Will to exist. Therefore, this world can only be one of misery. For Schopenhauer, two possible solutions exist to escape from such misery. A temporary solution is through art, in which one can detach oneself from the Will for a time by sharing in art's representation of the world of ideas. The only permanent solution to the world's misery, though, is through cultivating such an awareness of the suffering of existence that one loses all wish for existence and satisfaction.

Schopenhauer's generally pessimistic outlook, that human existence is primarily an existence of pain in which human beings constantly search for ways to alleviate the pain, manifests itself in Conrad's works in a number of ways: from Winnie's view in *The Secret Agent* that "things don't bear looking into very much" (138) to the absurdity of events that wreck Razumov's life in *Under Western Eyes*. Similarly, Conrad's recognition of the need for temporary shelter from the truths of an indifferent universe resembles Schopenhauer's idea about the need for respite from the pain of human existence.

Movements in art and literature

Any discussion of movements in art and literature should begin by recognizing that Conrad resisted being associated with any particular literary movement because he felt that it restricted and compartmentalized a writer's work. Nevertheless, one can still discuss certain tendencies in Conrad's work in light of the literary and artistic movements of his time, particularly since his own work was often instrumental in developing some of these movements. Among the literary and artistic movements of Conrad's time, Modernism was the most important to his work. Modernism is known for its formal experimentation. In fiction, this experimentation took a number of forms: achronological narratives, multiple narrators, stream-of-consciousness narration, fragmented narratives, inconclusive endings, unreliable narrators, and so on. Of course, some authors had previously experimented with certain of these techniques, but the Modernist period was the first in which experimentation took such a prominent position. There were several reasons for this phenomenon. In one sense, Modernist authors were simply representing in form what they perceived in fact, that is the fragmented forms these authors employed were meant to resemble the fragmented world they encountered. In another sense, though, the formal experimentation is a truly radical change in the history of the arts. Although all movements in the arts in some way react against earlier movements, form has typically been fairly constant. Sonnets, for instance, by William Wordsworth, Francis Petrarch, William Shakespeare, and Percy Bysshe Shelley may differ in the ideas they express and how they express them, but their one shared feature is that they employ the sonnet form. The Modernists, though, not only reacted against the conception of art espoused in previous movements, but they also reacted against the forms themselves. Of course, a certain amount of formal experimentation had been developing for some time. Wordsworth's insisting that the language of poetry should be the language of the average person and Walt Whitman's advocating free verse in poetry are just two examples. Nevertheless, the widespread view of making things new, as Ezra Pound demanded, was unique to the Modernists. A more profound reason, however, lies at the heart of these changes, that is that the formal changes mirrored the social changes. In a society in which even the long-held idea of the pre-eminence of Western civilization came into question, the pre-eminence of its artistic forms similarly came into question.

Modernism was not just concerned with formal experimentation, though. Modernist writers were just as concerned with larger philosophical issues. Modernist literature is often known for its insistence on an indifferent universe, for its alienation of the individual in the modern world, for its indeterminacy of knowledge, and for its emphasis on conceptions of the self. All of these come out of the atmosphere of uncertainty concerning traditionally held truths that arose in the nineteenth century. As a result, Modernist writers were forced to confront an indifferent universe in which no transcendent truths were available and yet still try to make sense of human existence.

Conrad is known primarily as a Modernist writer, and he certainly fits in with the movement. In fact, he may be the first Modernist. His works clearly evidence both the Modernist experimentation with form and the Modernist view of the world. Formal experimentation appears as early as his first novel, *Almayer's Folly*, with the flash back and flash forward techniques he employs. This experimentation becomes much more pronounced in many of the works from his middle period on. The shifts in time and space that occur in *Lord*

Jim and even more drastically in *Nostromo* are examples of the Conrad's experimentation, as are the multiple narrators he employs in relating the tales told in "Heart of Darkness," "Typhoon," and elsewhere. On the other hand, the alienation, solitude, and epistemological uncertainty that so many of his characters experience speaks of Conrad's Modernist world view, as they consistently try to find meaning and order in human existence while recognizing that such is never transcendent but merely contingent – merely a means to stave off chaos, anarchy, and nihilism.

For Conrad, this position is particularly difficult given his age and maturity at the time he began his literary career. Although the philosophical subtext of his works is thoroughly Modernist, Conrad was still largely a product of the nineteenth century. Consequently, a tension exists between his realization of a Modernist world and his wish that it were otherwise. This attitude appears prominently in the way various characters see the need to recognize the ultimate absurdity of human existence and the indifference of the universe, but at the same time to be able to shelter themselves from such knowledge.

Other literary and artistic movements that provide a context for Conrad's work include Romanticism, Realism, Naturalism, and Impressionism. Romanticism was a reaction against Neoclassicism and Enlightenment thinking. The movement began in the late eighteenth century and rejected the Neoclassical focus on reason, rationality, and order and instead emphasized individualism, emotion, subjectivity, and imagination. Romanticism is also closely associated with German Idealist philosophy, particularly through Coleridge's borrowing of Idealist concepts. Sometime during the nineteenth century, however, the movement became popularized, and an important distinction must be made regarding Romanticism and popularized Romanticism. Popularized Romanticism largely came out of the Romantic idea of the individual striving to go beyond limitations and the strains of Idealist philosophy contained in Romanticism. The result was a diluting of the original Romantic ideas, and Romanticism began to be associated with, for example, idealistic codes of behavior (as opposed to Idealist philosophy) and adventurous activity (as opposed to individualism and striving beyond limitations). Consequently, the term "Romantic" came to take on pejorative connotations and was roundly criticized by many in the late nineteenth and early twentieth centuries.

Romanticism, though, is perhaps the most interesting movement in relationship to Conrad's works. He was clearly influenced by some of the Polish Romantic writers of the early nineteenth century, such as Adam Mickiewicz and Julius Słowacki, as well as by his own father's Romantic writings. Having largely disappeared by the time of Conrad's birth, Romanticism was certainly long since rejected by the movements corresponding to Conrad's literary career. Romanticism is nevertheless an important element in much of Conrad's fiction, and his relationship to it is ambivalent. On the one hand, as evidenced in *Lord Jim*, Conrad is critical of actions and ideas that are motivated by Romantic impulses. At the same time, though, Conrad in part approves of such impulses. In other words, the idealism that Jim expresses is illusory, but it also causes him to strive beyond the mundane. It is what provides him with hope. And so Conrad was both attracted to and repelled by Romantic idealism. Furthermore, Conrad clearly approved of a code of honor and duty, but again his attitude toward them is mixed in that although he approved of such ideas, he did so not because he believed they resulted from transcendental ideals but rather because they provided for ordered and useful social interaction.

Realism and Naturalism were both reactions against Romanticism and were both movements born out of the philosophical and social issues of the nineteenth century, particularly the rise of science. Rather than representing an idealized view of the world, Realism tried to represent reality as it actually existed. For subject material, Realist writers focused more on observation than imagination, and they avoided exaggeration, poetic language, and melodramatic conventions. They wished to represent events and objects that any observer could recognize, ideally removing the variable of human subjectivity in the process. In this way, all readers were to experience the same thing, just as the scientist expects the results of a scientific experiment to be the same regardless of who performs it. Naturalism even more clearly looked to science as its model, as is evidenced in Émile Zola's reliance on the scientific methods of Claude Bernard to construct his naturalistic fiction. Naturalism advocated conforming as closely as possible to the natural world. Naturalist novels were typically novels of social conscience that dealt with the seamier side of civilization and the social problems of the modern world. They tended to work strongly from a Social Darwinist view of the world, that is they saw Darwin's idea of natural selection to be as active in the human world as it was in the animal world. Hence, heredity and environment were primary determinants in the outcome of an individual's life and circumstances.

Although Conrad clearly attempted to represent a real rather than ideal world in his fiction, his work largely reacts against the premises of Realism and Naturalism. The formal experimentation in his work stands in sharp contrast to the chronological and non-individualist fiction of Realism. Since Conrad focused strongly on the individual and since his works consistently represent all phenomena from the external world filtering through human consciousness, Realism's attempt to remove subjectivity from the representational process runs directly counter to Conrad's representation of reality. In the case of Naturalism, Conrad's work is even further removed. In the first place, his novels could not be considered novels of social conscience, as were so many Realist and Naturalist novels. Instead, Conrad's focus was on the struggles of the individual to find meaning in human existence. Furthermore, Conrad's suspicion of science as the source for certainty in the modern world would not allow him to accept the primary tenets of Realism and Naturalism. Finally, Naturalism's insistence on the almost all-encompassing influence of environment and heredity on an individual's fate runs counter to Conrad's view of the individual's relationship to the world.

In contrast, Impressionism was a particularly important movement to Conrad's work. Begun in the visual arts in the 1860s and 1870s, Impressionist painters focused on atmosphere, point of view, sharp juxtaposition of colors, innovative use of light, and the use of evocative brush strokes. They also sought to represent the interaction between human consciousness and the objects of that consciousness. Much of this interaction appears as sensory perception, particularly visual perception, but, with literary Impressionism at least, it would be wrong to limit this process solely to visual perception or even to sensory perception in general. Indeed, literary Impressionists represented a broad spectrum of objects of consciousness: physical objects, human subjects, events, ideas, space, and time.

Impressionism is sometimes misunderstood as the solely subjective responses of the artist to the object, but the relationship is really more of an exchange between artist and object. The representation of the object may show an object altered by the artist's impression of it, but the object is not wholly created by the artist. In other words, Impressionism runs a middle course between Realism and Surrealism. It seeks to represent a contextualized experience such that an object cannot be experienced except at a particular place, at a particular time, by a particular person. Impressionists were simply representing the idea that all phenomena filter through human consciousness.

In the case of Conrad, this relationship between subject and object appears in a variety of ways. In *The Shadow-Line*, for instance, the new captain views his first command differently from the way others view it. While others may see merely a mode of transport, the new captain sees the consummation of his many years' work. Similarly, in *The Secret Agent*, the time that Winnie experiences during Verloc's murder is altered by the context of that event: Winnie experiences the murder to have taken a much longer time than the clock registers. In both cases, as is true elsewhere in his works, Conrad represents phenomena being filtered through the consciousness of his characters, such that subject alters object, object alters subject, and both are influenced by the context in which they appear.

The numerous important events, issues, and other happenings of the late nineteenth and early twentieth centuries require one to consider them in any discussion of Modernist literature, and because of his unusually diverse experience, one must certainly consider them in any discussion of Conrad's works.

Chapter 3

Conrad's early period

Conrad's early period is dominated by narratives about the Malay Archipelago and the maritime profession. For this reason, Conrad was (and often still is) thought of as a sea writer. Conrad's early writings serve as a writer's apprenticeship of sorts. Often thought to be more uneven than the works of his middle period, these works nevertheless have much to recommend them, and when they were published they were well received by the critics.

Almayer's Folly

Almayer's Folly is Conrad's first novel, and the first of a reverse trilogy – that is the first written but the last in the chronology of events that take place in *The Rescue, An Outcast of the Islands,* and *Almayer's Folly*. The novel deals with Almayer, a trader in a remote region of the Malay Archipelago, who has married his mentor Tom Lingard's adopted Sulu daughter with the promise that one day he would become Lingard's heir. By the time the novel opens, though, Lingard has lost his money and disappeared to Europe, and Almayer's wife has retreated back to her cultural roots. Almayer's one hope is of becoming rich and leaving the East to return to Europe with his daughter, Nina. To this end, he has engaged Dain Maroola, a Balinese ruler, to help search for rumored gold. Unbeknownst to Almayer, Nina and Dain Maroola have fallen in love. Before Maroola and Almayer can begin their search for gold, however, the Dutch authorities arrive to arrest Maroola for seeking to overthrow Dutch rule. Maroola flees the Dutch, running off with Nina. When a slave girl tells Almayer what has happened, he intercepts the couple and tries to convince Nina to return. When she refuses, Almayer returns home a broken man, slipping into opium addiction and eventual death.

Almayer's Folly was considered a Romance when it was published, and to a certain extent it is, but Conrad plays with the Romance form. Unlike most Romances, the novel does not end happily, nor is the love interest of the typical sort or the exotic setting romanticized. Instead, Conrad turns the Romance form on its end, creating an entirely new kind of Romance. More than its form, though, the novel's content radically diverges from previous Romance fiction. Conrad presents the East as a place of squalor and political intrigue in which the Malayans outwit and ultimately destroy the European Almayer, who is overmatched in this environment and appears wholly ineffectual. Furthermore, Almayer's daughter, Nina, chooses her Malayan heritage over her European heritage. These events bring into question the Western view of the world, a trend that would become commonplace in so much of Conrad's subsequent fiction to follow. In *Almayer's Folly*, Conrad further undermines Western values through Almayer's Eurocentrism toward non-Westerners and through the Westerners' prejudicial treatment of the half European Nina. In the end, the novel posits the possibility that Nina is better off with Dain Maroola and her Malayan heritage than with Almayer living in Europe. Furthermore, the erosion of Almayer's position in Sambir as well as the erosion of his great unfinished house, dubbed "Almayer's Folly," becomes representative of an eroding European presence and power in colonial territories. In this way, Conrad's novel takes a politically radical turn in doubting the ascendency and role of Western civilization in the non-Western world. This is not to suggest that Conrad was devoid of European prejudice toward non-Westerners in the novel. In fact, one of the particularly interesting things about the novel is the way that the novel questions European assumptions about the non-Western world while at the same time perpetuating those same assumptions.

In addition to the novel's commentary on these larger social and political issues, Conrad sets an example that he continues throughout much of his work as he focuses on issues that affect individual lives. In other words, the larger social, political, and philosophical issues that Conrad addresses intertwine with the lives of individuals, demonstrating the individual consequences of such issues, and always individual lives take precedence. In *Almayer's Folly*, Conrad focuses on the lives of Almayer and Nina. Almayer's struggle is particularly poignant since he places all of his hope in the idea of growing wealthy and leaving the East with his daughter. His primary problem, though, is that he lives in the future – in a vision of luxury in Europe. As a result, when he discovers that Nina intends to run off with Maroola, his world collapses. With his future existence destroyed, he is left with nothing in the present, and despairs. Almayer is ill-equipped to deal with reality and graphically reveals the illusory nature of dreams. On the other hand, Nina struggles to fit into one or the other of the cultures that she inherits. With a Malayan mother and a European father, she is heir to both cultures but fits into neither. Brought up to be European by her father, she is not accepted in that community and eventually rejects her European heritage for her Malayan heritage. Thus, in addition to a choice that would have surprised most of Conrad's readers, Nina demonstrates a strength of character and will as she chooses her own fate rather than having others determine it for her. In this way, she shows herself to be the dominant force in the novel, a unique situation for a woman, particularly a non-Western woman. Consequently, the conclusion to *Almayer's Folly* is truly radical, as Conrad completely undermines the conventional social norms that appear in Romance fiction.

An Outcast of the Islands

An Outcast of the Islands is the second in Conrad's Malay trilogy. Again set in the Malay Archipelago, the action of the novel occurs before that of *Almayer's Folly* and focuses on Peter Willems, the outcast of the title. As a youth, he meets Tom Lingard, who accepts Willems as a protégé. With Lingard's help, Willems eventually rises to the position of clerk for Hudig & Co. Willems embezzles funds from the company to pay gambling debts and slowly repays the money. Just before he finishes repaying the sum, Hudig discovers what Willems has done, and fires him. Willems returns home, is berated by his half-caste wife, Joanna, and leaves. Shortly thereafter, Lingard chances upon Willems and decides to give him another chance, bringing him to the remote trading outpost in Sambir where Almayer lives. Lingard has developed a trading monopoly because he knows a secret route to Sambir. While there, Willems tires of the situation. He meets Aïssa, the daughter of a former Brunei leader, and, feeling that he has been wronged by his wife, Hudig, Lingard, Almayer, and his entire community, Willems takes up with her and betrays Lingard's secret passage to Syed Abdulla, an Arab trader, thus breaking Lingard's monopoly. Returning again to Sambir, Lingard goes to Willems, whom Abdulla has cast off now that he is no longer useful, and confronts Willems with his betrayal, but Willems blames his actions on Aïssa's influence over him. Ignoring this excuse, Lingard refuses to have anything further to do with him and refuses to help Willems leave Sambir. Shortly afterwards, wary of Willems's proximity, Almayer arranges to have Willems's wife and son sent to him from Almayer's trading post where Lingard had left them. After they arrive and Aïssa realizes that Willems is married and wants to leave her, a struggle ensues in which Willems tries to take his gun from Aïssa but is shot and killed.

Although *An Outcast of the Islands* is a remarkable book, many would not consider it to be one of Conrad's best novels. It is not an artistic masterpiece, but it is remarkable because of its innovations. In the novel, Conrad questions colonial attitudes, undermines the Romance tradition, and creates perhaps the first true anti-hero in the British novel.

As he did in *Almayer's Folly*, in *An Outcast of the Islands*, Conrad inverts the traditional Romance novel. The novel does not end happily, the exotic setting is not idyllic, and Abdulla, not Willems or Lingard, is the victor at the end of the novel. Conrad further undermines the Romance by choosing an anti-hero for his main character. Willems is an anti-hero not only because he acts unheroically but also because he is thoroughly despicable, and yet he is the center of the novel's events and of the novel's focus.

More than simply to invert the Romance form, though, Conrad creates an anti-hero in order to investigate the nature of moral rectitude. To this end, Willems's betrayals are particularly important. In his history of betrayal, Willems is guilty of one of the most significant crimes in Conrad's world. Because Conrad refuses to posit absolute truths, moral rectitude is based upon the mutual acceptance of communal morals by its members. The ideas of community and solidarity are important to Conrad because they provide for physical and psychological comfort. When an individual betrays others, the sole thread holding the individual to society is cut. Because Willems betrays so many bonds (employer/employee, husband/wife, etc.), Lingard says to him, "You are not fit to go amongst people" (275), and thus Willems must bear the role of outcast. Furthermore, Willems refuses to accept responsibility for his actions and consistently blames others for his failings. Rather than blaming himself for getting fired, he blames Hudig. Rather than blaming himself for the ensuing argument with his wife, Joanna, he blames her. Rather than blaming himself for betraying Lingard, he blames Aïssa. Finally, when he betrays Aïssa, intending to leave her and return to his wife, he again justifies himself by saying that Aïssa "is sin" (278). In each case, he sees himself in the right, wholly justified in his actions. Willems's death at the end of the novel is simply the physical manifestation of his already existing moral state.

In addition to the moral issues that Conrad investigates, a prominent issue in the novel is colonialism, as Conrad questions Western assumptions about race. Willems becomes Conrad's vehicle in investigating these issues. Besides his self-absorption and belief in his own merits, Willems believes that he merits privileged status because he is European, and he tries to trade upon his position as a white man. He denigrates Joanna, Aïssa, and the Malayans in general. Conrad writes that Willems believed that he would be able "to tyrannize good-humouredly over his half-caste wife, to notice with tender contempt his pale yellow child, to patronize loftily his dark-skinned brother-in-law" (3). Willems enjoys his privileged status:

> That family's admiration was the great luxury of his life. It rounded and completed his existence in a perpetual assurance of unquestionable superiority. He loved to breathe the coarse incense they offered before the shrine of the successful white man; the man that had done them the honour to marry their daughter, sister, cousin.   (3–4)

Willems's superiority, however, is illusory. His wife's family may pay homage to him, but the morally bankrupt life that Willems leads undercuts his status. In addition, his moral state undermines his racial superiority and also the general feeling of the time concerning the absolute superiority of whites over non-whites. Willems is in no way superior to the non-Westerners in the novel. Both the Westerners and non-Westerners recognize this fact; once Abdulla no longer needs Willems, he quickly discards him as dangerous and unhealthy.

Conrad further investigates the question of colonialism through the attitudes of both the Western and non-Western characters toward colonial activity. All of the Westerners who interact with the non-Westerners consider them with either contempt or condescension. Almayer, for instance, considers his wife to be a degraded individual and has little regard for any of the other non-Westerners he encounters. At one point, Almayer complains that Lingard jeopardized him by helping some Chinese: "And then three months afterwards you go and do that mad trick – for a lot of Chinamen too. Chinamen!" (162). On the other hand, Lingard's attitude is more condescending than contemptuous, but he nevertheless sees himself as superior to non-Westerners. Conrad relates that Lingard "had been living with Malays so long and so close that the extreme deliberation and deviousness of their mental proceedings had ceased to irritate him much" (222). Later, he says to Babalatchi, "If I ever spoke to Patalolo, like an elder brother, it was for your good – for the good of all" (226). What we discover during the course of the novel, though, is that the Westerners seem to behave no better than the non-Westerners. Babalatchi points this out:

> You think it is only your wisdom and your virtue and your happiness that are true. You are stronger than the wild beasts, but not so wise. A black tiger knows when he is not hungry – you do not. He knows the difference between himself and those that can speak; you do not understand the difference between yourselves and us – who are men.   (226)

Later, Babalatchi berates Lingard, saying, "I have learned much wisdom this morning. There are no men anywhere. You whites are cruel to your friends and merciful to your enemies – which is the work of fools" (240). The primary argument behind the colonial endeavor was that non-Westerners would benefit from the dissemination of Western values and ideas. In the novel, though, the opposite seems to be the case. Not only do non-Westerners not benefit from Western values, Western civilization actually becomes detrimental to them. In showing this, Conrad takes a subversive stance against the popular Western view of colonialism. In the example of Willems's moral degeneracy and in the example of the Western role in the Malay Archipelago, Conrad demonstrates that status is not bestowed by one's heritage but rather by one's moral action.

The Rescue

The Rescue is a difficult novel to place in Conrad's career. Begun in the late 1890s, it was not completed until some twenty-three years later and was finally published in 1920. As a result, it could be considered part of Conrad's later career or part of his earlier career. Since Conrad wrote a good deal of the novel during his early period and since *The Rescue* constitutes the third in the Malay trilogy and many of the issues in the novel resemble those Conrad addressed earlier rather than later in his career, the novel will be considered here alongside the other two in the trilogy.

The Rescue takes up again the scene of *Almayer's Folly* and *An Outcast of the Islands*, but the action of the novel occurs chronologically before that of *An Outcast of the Islands* and deals extensively with Tom Lingard as a young man. Because Hassim, a local Malayan ruler, had saved Lingard's life, Lingard repays the debt by saving from death Hassim, his sister, and a few of Hassim's followers after Hassim has been ousted as ruler by a rival party. Having spirited Hassim and his followers away, Lingard deposits them at a place called the shore of refuge with the idea of later helping Hassim reclaim his position. Lingard spends several years preparing arms and allies for the attempt. This process requires delicate and tenuous alliances among several parties, and just as the preparations are coming to fruition a sailing yacht called the *Hermit*, owned by a Mr. Travers, becomes stranded in the vicinity of the alliance's headquarters. As a result of a number of misunderstandings, brought about by the mutual mistrust of seemingly all parties involved, two of the men from the yacht are captured as hostages. Lingard negotiates their release into his custody, but in the meantime Carter, who has been left in charge of Lingard's brig, feels threatened and sinks some of the Malayan boats. This act brings about a crisis of trust among the various parties. One faction attempts to capture Lingard's store of arms and trade that are meant for the struggle to reinstate Hassim. Unable to resist and unable to communicate with Lingard, who has gone to try to repair the damaged alliance, Jörgenson, Lingard's assistant, blows up the store of arms, taking with him those who had sought to capture the *Emma* where the arms had been stored. In the process, Hassim and his sister, who had been captured as hostages, are also killed.

With the exception of *Nostromo*, *The Rescue* is the longest of Conrad's novels. Given the time it took for Conrad to write it, one might expect *The Rescue* to be one of Conrad's most polished products, but that is not the case. *The Rescue* has its moments, and it deals with some important issues in Conrad's thought, but it also lacks the polish and power of some of his other works. Nevertheless, the novel merits discussion and gains in value when considered alongside the other novels in the trilogy and alongside Conrad's other early Malay fiction.

The issue that permeated Conrad's early works, that is the relationship between East and West, is one of the major ideas that Conrad considers in *The Rescue*. Hassim's actions toward Lingard and Lingard's actions toward Hassim are generous and free from racial prejudice. Both individuals care deeply for one another, and each goes to considerable effort and risk for the other's benefit. That said, though, *The Rescue* may be Conrad's most pessimistic investigation into the possible accord between Westerners and non-Westerners because, despite Hassim's and Lingard's feelings toward one another, they cannot break through the inherited racial barrier that ultimately divides them. In the end, Lingard chooses to aid Travers and company rather than Hassim. In fact, Conrad further emphasizes this barrier by presenting Hassim as eminently worthy of Lingard's aid and Travers and company as eminently unworthy of his aid. This barrier is even more apparent among the other Westerners and non-Westerners that people the novel. The non-Westerners, even Hassim, do not understand or trust those aboard the *Hermit*. They do not know why they are there, and they do not understand Travers and company's relationship to Lingard. This is why they are suspicious and take the steps they do, capturing the two men as hostages, then later taking Hassim and his sister hostage, and finally attempting to capture the *Emma*. At the same time, the Westerners are equally distrustful of the non-Westerners. They see them as intriguing and inferior, which is one reason why Carter sinks the Malayan boats. As a result, what amounts to several misunderstandings that probably could have been cleared up had they occurred among one group or the other become disastrous when they occur between the Westerners and non-Westerners.

This situation is further exacerbated by the fact that the different factions in both groups mistrust one another. For instance, Lingard's mistrust of Travers and his crew (except Mrs. Travers) causes him to withhold his intentions from them; this results in Carter's sinking the boats, which heralds the downfall of the tenuous alliance Lingard had constructed. Similarly, Jörgenson's mistrust of Mrs. Travers causes him to withhold the meaning of the ring she is to carry to Lingard warning of Hassim's capture, and Mrs. Travers's mistrust of Lingard causes her to withhold giving the ring to him, the final blow that brings down Lingard's house-of-cards alliance. In the same way, the mistrust and competition among the several Malayan factions causes them to take more resolute steps than they would otherwise have done. This pervasive atmosphere of mistrust results in a situation hopelessly doomed from the outset.

The tragic events of *The Rescue*, though, go beyond the confines of the novel. Conrad is also commenting on the nature of communal relationships in general. In many ways, for Conrad, the plight of Lingard's alliances is the plight of humanity. In a world without absolute truths, communal ties exist not according to eternal laws but solely according to mutual trust, a trust as tenuous as the alliances Lingard cultivates. Ultimately, any human community can survive only through the mutual trust of its members. The fate of Lingard's alliances is the fate of all human communities when mistrust pervades.

Linked to the mistrust in *The Rescue* is the idea of betrayal. All of the novel's action has betrayal at its core. A faction of Hassim's people rebels against him, betraying him and wresting his rule from him. Similarly, Lingard's betrayal of Hassim in coming to the aid of the *Hermit* and Mrs. Travers's betrayal of Lingard by withholding the ring, along with the perceived betrayals of Lingard by Daman when he takes Mr. Travers and Mr. d'Alcacer captive and of Daman by Lingard when Carter sinks Daman's boats, all combine to bring about the disaster that ends the hope of restoring Hassim to power and results in the death of Hassim, Jörgenson, and so many others. In this way, *The Rescue* graphically represents the results of betrayal. In the end, Lingard recognizes that he has betrayed Hassim by protecting the members of the *Hermit*. To a certain extent, though, Lingard is placed in an extremely difficult position. He feels a moral obligation toward Hassim and his followers, but at the same time racial (and perhaps to a lesser extent moral) obligations require him to protect the passengers of the *Hermit*. It seems that he cannot remain loyal to both parties.

If the situation were as simple as this, one could simply pity Lingard for finding himself in an impossible position in which he cannot avoid betraying one party or the other. Conrad, however, further complicates the situation by introducing the romance between Lingard and Mrs. Travers. The reader then must wonder how much Lingard's actions are influenced by his conflicting loyalties and how much they are influenced by his attraction to Mrs. Travers. In adding this twist to the problem, Conrad questions Lingard's motivation and moral rectitude, but he also introduces the issue of women in the world of men. So often in Conrad's works, when women enter the male world they tend to disrupt a tenuous communal alliance. For Conrad perhaps, because communal alliances exist only by mutual agreement among members, any outside element inevitably disrupts a delicate balance. As a result, women tend to pose a threat to the male community Conrad establishes. Certainly, in *The Rescue*, Mrs. Travers's arrival in Lingard's male world brings disastrous consequences.

The Nigger of the "Narcissus"

The unfortunately titled *The Nigger of the "Narcissus"* (titled *Children of the Sea* in the first American edition) is Conrad's best work of his early period. In fact, were it not for the book's title, it undoubtedly would be read more often than it is currently. At one time, it was one of Conrad's most frequently read books. In part because of its brevity, in part because of its adventure qualities, and in part because of its literary qualities, the novel used to attract a good deal of attention.

The novel begins in Bombay with the crew assembling for their voyage back to England aboard the *Narcissus*. James Wait, a sailor of African descent, is the last crew member to arrive. Shortly after setting sail, Wait claims to be sick and unable to perform his duties. The crew is unsure whether he is actually ill or merely feigning illness. The men alternately cater to Wait and resent him, and he in turn tyrannizes over them. The other disruptive element among the crew is Donkin, who never accepts responsibility for his actions and consistently tries to shirk his duties. While rounding the Cape of Good Hope, the ship encounters a powerful storm and is nearly sunk. During the storm, the men make a desperate attempt to rescue Wait from his cabin and barely escape with their lives, for which trouble Wait berates them for taking so long. The ship eventually rights itself, and they continue on their voyage. At one point, Podmore the evangelical ship's cook, attempts to save Wait's soul, after which Wait, frightened by the implication of his impending death, declares himself fit for duty. Having had to put up with Wait claiming illness the entire trip, Captain Allistoun refuses to accept this change of heart. His decision leads to a near riot, incited by Donkin, during which Donkin throws a belaying pin at Allistoun and then tries to hide his act. After this act, the rest of the crew shun Donkin. Although Wait may have been feigning the extent of his illness, it turns out that he actually has been ill. In fact, he eventually dies of his illness and is buried at sea, at which point a breeze appears, and the ship makes the last leg of its trip to England. They arrive in England, and as the crew disembarks the bond that had held them dissolves.

The narrative technique of the novel has evoked much commentary because of its instability. Whether this is a mistake or deliberate is impossible to tell, but, regardless, an incongruity appears between what at some times seems to be an omniscient third-person narrative and at other times a first-person narrative. The narrator often reveals information that only an omniscient narrator could know, but at other times the narrator clearly appears to be an active participant in the events of the novel. Most readers find such instability awkward and see it as an artistic flaw.

Despite the narrative instability, the novel ushers in important issues that would inform all of Conrad's most significant work. In particular, Conrad deals with the concepts of human isolation and human solidarity. The novel is a paean to the community aboard ship, a community that provides comfort and safety for its members but also a community that resembles the plight of humanity everywhere. On board the *Narcissus*, Conrad creates a microcosm of the world as a whole. The men are isolated from the rest of humanity, and they exist in the midst of the hostile environment of the sea. In order to survive, they must establish their own community. The men appear to be mostly strangers to one another and must find a way to interact. During their voyage together, they recognize that they must cooperate in order to survive. In particular, the men must work together during the storm; otherwise, they would certainly perish. Their plight serves as a paradigm for humanity in general in which Conrad believes human beings need to work together to deal with the world around them. Confronted by a universe indifferent to the fate of humanity, Conrad sees human solidarity as the only means to protect oneself from dangers and perhaps the only means of making sense of the world.

In addition to the physical cooperation necessary to save the men's lives during the storm, social cooperation provides them with psychological comfort. In order to avoid human isolation, the men must form a community, a community that will give meaning to their existence and provide companionship in their lives. In particular, Conrad demonstrates the necessity of cooperation for the well being of the community by showing what happens when that cooperation is absent. Donkin demonstrates this lack most clearly. His selfish behavior during the storm leaves the men shorthanded and puts all of them in greater danger as a result, and his continued selfishness threatens the community of the crew by causing dissension among them and between the crew and the officers. Finally, when threatened with exposure, Donkin seeks to repudiate his role and instead tries to displace his guilt onto the crew as a whole. Similarly, Wait's selfish behavior threatens the community, as he causes the men alternately to support his illness and to begrudge his removal from the ship's daily routine. He further threatens the community because he becomes a constant reminder of death, both in his continual claims that he is dying (which the men often do not believe) and in his actual death. In each case, the men are forced to confront their own mortality and the disquieting effects of those thoughts. With the graphic examples of Donkin and Wait, Conrad effectively causes his readers to recognize the tenuous nature of human existence and to recognize the necessity of community for physical and psychological survival.

In addition to the major themes of human isolation and solidarity, the novel also obliquely considers questions of race. The importance of the communal bond among the men is clear in the novel, but the fact that Wait is of African heritage thrusts the men into something of a dilemma. On the one hand, Wait must be included in the community of the ship, but on the other hand, because of his heritage, he remains outside their larger social community. The conflict between these situations causes a tension in the way the men react to Wait. They seek to protect him as they would any other crew member, even going so far as to risk their lives for him, but they also exhibit an aversion to him, in part because he represents death to them but also in part because of racial prejudice.

Tales of Unrest

Tales of Unrest is Conrad's first collection of stories. It is a geographically mixed collection with two stories set in the Malay Archipelago, two set in Europe, and one set in Africa. As was often (but not always) the case with Conrad's short fiction, these stories are typically thought to have less literary merit than some of Conrad's other works, although they do deal with some issues that are particularly important to Conrad.

"The Idiots" is set in Brittany and is the tale of the plight of Susan Bacadou and her husband Jean-Pierre in bearing four mentally challenged children. When Jean-Pierre attempts to force Susan sexually in order to try to conceive a normal child, Susan stabs him with a pair of scissors, killing him. Rejected by her mother and believing she is being pursued by her husband's ghost, Susan flees toward the coast, where she falls into the sea and drowns. The story is of interest for two reasons: its comment on women's rights within marriage and its introduction of narrative innovation. Conrad first broaches the idea of the role of women in this story in which no mitigating circumstances seem open to Susan for killing Jean-Pierre. Susan's mother has no sympathy for her plight, and presumably the local authorities would concur. Society rejects Susan's right to protect herself from her husband's forcing himself upon her. In regards to sexual matters, she is Jean-Pierre's property in the eyes of society, and although society may have been morally offended by Jean-Pierre's actions, he did nothing illegal. Conrad clearly sympathizes with Susan and critiques a society in which she is not allowed to defend herself.

Conrad's narrative technique is also of interest in this story as he introduces a technique that Ian Watt coined "delayed decoding." Near the end of the story, Millot sees the ground pull out from underneath Susan's feet as she falls into the sea, and only after a moment or two does he recognize that Susan fell from an unmoving cliff. This narrative technique has two purposes. First, it places the reader in the position of the character viewing the event so that the reader experiences what the character does at the very moment that character experiences it, thus providing a realism and immediacy to the reader's experience. Second, delayed decoding emphasizes the tenuous nature of human perception, demonstrating that what one experiences filters through one's consciousness and hence is subjective and not objective. Furthermore, by emphasizing the subjectivity of perception, Conrad calls into question the certainty of knowledge obtained through perception, and hence, because so much knowledge results from empirical experience, by extension, this technique also calls into question the certainty of knowledge in general. Delayed decoding appears again and again in the course of Conrad's career and becomes one of his most important narrative innovations.

"Karain" and "The Lagoon" are both set in the Malay Archipelago, and both consider the issue of betrayal. "The Lagoon" is a story about a Malayan man, Arsat, who runs off with the servant woman of a local ruler. He is accompanied by his brother, and they are pursued by the ruler's guards. Arsat's brother offers to hold off the guards to give the couple time to prepare for the escape. Arsat is to wait for his brother, but fearful that there will not be enough time for them all to escape, he leaves his brother to die. The story is about the remorse Arsat feels for his betrayal. After the woman dies some years later, Arsat is left only with his guilt. He chooses the woman over his brother out of selfishness and in the end is left alone and isolated because of his choice. Of further interest is that Arsat tells his tale to a European trader, and in this tale, as occurs in so many others set in the Malay Archipelago, Conrad reveals the intersection of the Western and non-Western worlds. The European trader is friendly with Arsat, but his condescension is clear. The tale reveals Arsat's guilt and passion, which transcend geographical and cultural boundaries, but the European does not see these. In this fact, Conrad reveals the myopia of the Western view of the non-Western world.

"Karain: A Memory" is the more elaborate of the two tales. Like "The Lagoon," "Karain" considers the theme of betrayal and the relationship between the Western and non-Western worlds. Also like "The Lagoon," "Karain" is one of Conrad's earliest frame narratives, albeit a more sophisticated one that anticipates Conrad's later important frame narratives. In this story, Karain has been trading with English gun runners in his war against the Spanish. One night, he swims to the English boat and asks for asylum in England in order to escape the evil spirit that haunts him. Many years earlier, the sister of Karain's friend Matara ran off with a Dutch trader. Karain and Matara spent many years and endured much hardship in tracking the woman, determined to kill her and the Dutch trader in order to avenge the family's lost honor. In the process, Karain developed a strange obsession for the woman, and when they discovered the couple Karain killed Matara rather than allow him to kill the woman. Karain believed that his elderly servant kept Matara's spirit away, but when the servant dies Karain has no protection, and so he asks the English traders to take him away. The traders give him a makeshift talisman made from a jubilee coin with a picture of Queen Victoria. Karain takes this talisman and leaves believing that it will ward off Matara's spirit. Like "The Lagoon," "Karain" deals with how an individual copes with his memory of betrayal. Unlike Arsat, though, Karain's guilt appears as a spirit that haunts him. Both carry the weight of their guilt, however, and both remain exiles from their homes as a result of their betrayals. In "Karain," the intersection of Western and non-Western cultures also plays an important role. First, when the Dutch trader disregards local custom and runs off with Matara's sister, he reveals his Western arrogance toward non-Western cultures. More important, though, his actions ultimately bring about Matara's death and Karain's haunting and exile. The English traders exhibit a similar attitude. Like the European trader in "The Lagoon," the English traders in "Karain" are condescending toward Karain, and as in "The Lagoon," their inability to sympathize with the great guilt and fear that Karain feels reveals their insensitivity and racial bias. As happens in so many of the early Malay fictions, Conrad criticizes Western attitudes of superiority.

"The Return" has been roundly criticized, many commentators regarding it as Conrad's worst work of fiction, and Conrad himself seems not to have regarded it highly. Despite the generally negative evaluations, the issue of human connection in the modern world is worth noting in the story. "The Return" begins with Alvan Hervey returning home from work one evening to find that his wife of five years has left him for another man. Shortly thereafter, however, his wife, unable to go through with her decision, returns home. During their ensuing discussion, Hervey discovers that his wife has returned solely out of fear of the social scandal. He further discovers that human connection is crucial and that his wife has no connection for him or anyone else. Realizing this intolerable situation, Hervey suddenly leaves, presumably never to return.

"The Return" marks a departure from Conrad's earlier settings and characters and shows his ability to work outside his experience in the East. More important, though, the story presents a vision of indeterminacy, as Hervey comes to realize, "Nothing could be foreseen, foretold – guarded against" (159–60). During the course of the story, Hervey's preconceived notions concerning the rectitude of Western civilized ideas are shattered, and so he finally latches onto the one idea that he regards as a saving grace when he thinks, "Faith! – Love! – the undoubting, clear faith in the truth of a soul – the great tenderness . . . It was what he had wanted all his life" (178). To connect with another person provides hope for Hervey. This hope, however, eludes him when he realizes that his wife "had no love and no faith for any one. To give her your thought, your belief, was like whispering your confession over the edge of the world. Nothing came back – not even an echo" (183). This discovery causes Hervey to despair, as he realizes that in the modern world he is utterly alone. "The Return" has its weaknesses, but it addresses in a significant way an issue that will occupy Conrad's most important works.

"An Outpost of Progress" is the most accomplished story in this collection. Drawn from Conrad's own experience in the Congo, it explicitly questions European colonial activities. "An Outpost of Progress" has been compared to "Heart of Darkness," and they share many of the same elements, specifically the moral degeneration engendered by isolation and the nature of the dissemination of Western civilization. In addition, Conrad's sustained irony anticipates the controlled irony he will later display in *The Secret Agent*.

In the story, Kayerts and Carlier take charge of a trading post in the heart of the African jungle. They go there hoping to become wealthy through trading ivory, but they also see themselves as ambassadors of progress in propagating Western values. At one point in the story, in exchange for ivory, Makola, Kayerts's and Carlier's assistant, sells into slavery some of the African workers at the station. Initially, Kayerts and Carlier are scandalized by the idea, but eventually they cover up Makola's action. Later in the story, while the men fight over some sugar, Kayerts accidentally shoots and kills Carlier. When Kayerts hears the company steamboat approaching the station, he hangs himself.

Rather than becoming wealthy or becoming catalysts for progress, the men become examples of moral and cultural degeneration, and far from being an outpost of progress, the station becomes one of regress. From the beginning, Conrad presents Kayerts and Carlier as ineffectual and incompetent, but more than that, in the slave trading incident and in the sugar incident, Conrad emphasizes the moral degradation of these ambassadors of Western civilization. Removed from the strictures and support of Western civilization, the men grow increasingly more uncivilized. Furthermore, in Europe, colonialism was justified because the colonizers were disseminating civilized progress to the uncivilized world, thereby benefiting the indigenous peoples. Instead of bringing progress to the Africans, however, Kayerts's and Carlier's presence is detrimental, since the relationship between the Europeans and the local people deteriorates significantly during the course of the story. Even more important, the local community is devastated by Makola's slave trading, and the final statement of "An Outpost of Progress" unrelentingly indicts Western colonial activity.

With the completion of *Tales of Unrest*, Conrad was ready to move on to the next phase of his career, in which he would produce some of the finest works of literature of the twentieth century.

Chapter 4

Conrad's middle period

Conrad is best known for the writings of his middle period, which ranges from approximately 1899 to 1911. This period was Conrad's most productive and has generally been seen as comprising his most artistically accomplished works. Certainly, he wrote his most frequently read and frequently studied works during this period.

"Youth" and Two Other Stories

"Youth" is one of Conrad's best short stories and is the first of four tales ("Youth," "Heart of Darkness," *Lord Jim,* and *Chance*) in which Charlie Marlow serves as the chief narrator. The story is a frame narrative in which Marlow tells his tale to several listeners, one of whom records the tale, acting as frame narrator. Marlow tells his listeners about an experience he had some twenty years earlier. He had just joined the crew as second mate of the *Judea,* bound for Bankok with a cargo of coal. From the outset, the journey is beset with difficulties. They leave London for Newcastle to collect their cargo but encounter bad weather and arrive late. More delays occur, including the *Judea* being hit by another vessel. Finally, setting off some three months after leaving London, the *Judea* again encounters bad weather in the English Channel and begins leaking, forcing yet another delay of several months while they await repairs. After the repairs are completed, the *Judea* finally sets off for its original destination. The ship encounters no more problems until it gets near Java Head, when the crew discovers a fire in the cargo hold. They are forced to pump water into the hold to try to put out the fire. They believe they have succeeded, when the ship suddenly explodes. A nearby mailboat attempts to tow the *Judea,* but the fire grows worse, and the crew is forced to abandon ship. They escape in the lifeboats, one of which Marlow commands. After watching the ship sink, the crew members in the boats head for land. Many hours later, they reach land at night. Marlow's tale ends with his awakening the next morning to his first view of the exotic East.

As the title suggests, the story concerns the issue of youth and those ideas and feelings associated with it. The story's primary value is in the irony Conrad achieves in having an older Marlow relate and comment upon his actions and feelings as a young man. Some commentators have seen the story as a paean to youth, and the story is certainly that, as Marlow recounts his youthful exuberance. The young Marlow's excitement and wonder at what he experiences resurrect pleasant memories in Marlow, his listeners, and presumably Conrad's readers as well. Even the young Marlow's ignorance and naïveté are remembered fondly and evoke pleasant emotions in Marlow's listeners. The tale and the memory, though, are also bittersweet because they invoke a time and state of mind and emotion that have disappeared into the past, never to be recovered.

Furthermore, in the background of this tale of youth lies the inevitable movement toward old age and death. Images of aging and death abound: the aging captain, his aging wife, the aging first mate, the aging ship, even Marlow's aging clothes, and by the time Marlow tells his tale all are dead, including his own youth: "youth, strength, genius, thoughts, achievements, simple hearts – all die . . . No matter" (7).

Conrad evokes the wonder of youth as he narrates his responses to his surroundings as a young man. The *Judea*'s motto is "Do or Die," and Marlow remarks, "I remember it took my fancy immensely. There was a touch of romance in it, something that made me love the old thing – something that appealed to my youth!" (5). When Marlow finally reaches land in the lifeboat, he is filled with wonder:

> And this is how I see the East. I have seen its secret places and have looked into its very soul; but now I see it always from a small boat, a high outline of mountains, blue and afar in the morning; like faint mist at noon; a jagged wall of purple at sunset . . . We drag at the oars with aching arms, and suddenly a puff of wind, a puff faint and tepid and laden with strange odours of blossoms, of aromatic wood, comes out of the still night – the first sigh of the East on my face. That I can never forget. It was impalpable and enslaving, like a charm, like a whispered promise of mysterious delight.   (37)

The older Marlow tells his listeners, "But for me all the East is contained in that vision of my youth. It is all in that moment when I opened my young eyes on it" (42). However, Marlow remembers his first experience with the East with a touch of sadness. He recognizes the naïveté of his view of the world as a youth and can laugh at it, but he also feels regret:

I remember my youth and the feeling that will never come back any more – the feeling that I could last for ever, outlast the sea, the earth, and all men; the deceitful feeling that lures us on to joys, to perils, to love, to vain effort – to death; the triumphant conviction of strength, the heat of life in the handful of dust, the glow in the heart that with every year grows dim, grows cold, grows small, and expires – and expires, too soon – before life itself.   (36–7)

Marlow's listeners also experience mixed emotions as they remember their own youths, as the frame narrator concludes the story by saying, "our faces marked by toil, by deceptions, by success, by love; our weary eyes looking still, looking always, looking anxiously for something out of life, that while it is expected is already gone – has passed unseen, in a sigh, in a flash – together with the youth, with the strength, with the romance of illusions" (42); and although this story contains none of the bitterness of old age, it faithfully represents the nostalgia and sadness of a lost youth and a clear awareness of an inexorable death.

"Heart of Darkness" is a dark, densely packed, and slow-moving story about a journey up the Congo River, in which Conrad investigates colonialism, self-knowledge, and the groundings of Western civilization. The story is loosely based upon Conrad's own experience in the Congo, and he notes in the "Author's Preface" that the story "is experience pushed a little (and only very little) beyond the actual facts of the case" (xi). There is no doubt that Conrad's own experience in the Congo had a profound affect on him; he is reputed to have once told Edward Garnett, "Before the Congo I was just a mere animal," and it is this effect that Conrad tries to transmit to his readers.

The story begins with four men sitting on the deck of the *Nellie*, anchored on the river Thames and waiting for the tide to change. Among them is an unnamed frame narrator, who recounts the tale that Marlow tells them. Marlow had been having trouble finding work when he finally got command of a steamboat on the Congo river and sets off on his journey to Africa. When he arrives at the company's Outer Station, he finds a combination of waste and decay. He leaves shortly thereafter for the company's Central Station to take command of his steamboat. Upon arriving, he finds his steamboat sunk and is forced to wait several months for repairs, after which Marlow and the others finally set off up river for the company's Inner Station to relieve Kurtz, the station manager there. Just below the station, they are attacked by Africans, during which Marlow's African helmsman is killed. Expecting to find the Inner Station destroyed, they are surprised to discover it intact. Marlow meets the Russian there, a disciple of Kurtz, who confidentially informs Marlow that Kurtz has taken a seat as one of the local deities among the Africans and that he had ordered the attack because he did not want to be taken back down river. Kurtz, who had been ill for some time, dies during the return voyage, his last words being "The horror! The horror!" Marlow also falls ill and barely escapes with his life, after which he is sent back to Europe. Before Kurtz died, a subtle bond had developed between Marlow and Kurtz, and Kurtz entrusted Marlow with some letters and papers. After recovering from his illness, Marlow decides to return a thin packet of letters from Kurtz's fiancée (his Intended). While visiting her, it becomes clear that she knows only the idealistic Kurtz who set out for Africa, not the one who was worshiped like a god. At one point, Marlow lets slip that he had heard Kurtz's last words. Upon learning this, the still grieving woman demands that Marlow tell them to her. After some hesitation, he tells her that Kurtz's last words were her name and then leaves. Marlow concludes by telling his listeners that he could not bring himself to tell her the truth.

"Heart of Darkness" is Conrad's most well-known story, in which he considers such significant issues as the nature of human existence and the nature of the universe. The story is also Conrad's first attempt to implement fully the narrative methods with which he had been experimenting in his previous fiction: frame narrative, multiple narrators, achronological narrative, and delayed decoding. Conrad had already used frame narratives in other stories, but in "Heart of Darkness" he expands the narrator's role such that a disparity arises between Marlow's view of events and the frame narrator's (at least at the beginning of the story). These disparate views provide the impetus for the story, but they also serve to present contrasting points of view. This effect is augmented by Conrad's use of multiple narrators. He would refine this technique in later works, but even in "Heart of Darkness" Conrad presents different information from different sources. Similarly, the narrative chronology Conrad employs is unique. As early as *Almayer's Folly*, Conrad had experimented with narrative chronology, but not until "Heart of Darkness" does he introduce a truly unique variation. The chronology of the story is a direct indirection, in which Marlow appears to tell a chronological tale but in fact does not. The narrative proceeds not according to the sequence of events but according to the sequence of Marlow's thoughts. Almost invariably when Marlow mentions women, for example, it is not when they actually appear in the story but rather when he happens to think of them. Finally, Conrad had used delayed decoding in some of his earlier works, and it appears prominently in "Heart of Darkness," again in a more fully developed form, when during the attack, for instance, Marlow initially sees sticks flying about and only afterwards sees those objects as arrows.

Conrad also returns to a fuller investigation of important ideas that he had considered in his previous works. Early in the story, the frame narrator comments on the famous adventurers and conquerors who had set forth from the Thames. The narrator's laudatory description of these past adventurers causes Marlow to contrast contemporary England with the England that the Romans encountered when they came to conquer it some two thousand years earlier. Thus begins Marlow's inquiry into the basic assumptions about Western civilization of the frame narrator and the other men on board, as well as those of Conrad's reading public. At the time of the story's writing, England was the most wealthy and powerful nation on earth. It was also the epicenter of Western civilization and represented the height of civilized progress, and London, where the *Nellie* is anchored, was the pinnacle of English society as well as the literal and symbolic source from which civilized progress issued forth to the rest of the world. Marlow, however, points out that to the conquering Romans the British would have been mere savages and Britain a mere wilderness. In fact, Marlow's description of the England that the Romans would have encountered seems strikingly similar to the description of the Congo that Marlow gives later in the story. Marlow does suggest a distinction between the Roman conquerors and the European colonizers, arguing that the Romans' rule "was merely a squeeze . . . They grabbed what they could get for the sake of what was to be got," while of the Europeans he says, "What saves us is efficiency – the devotion to efficiency" (50). Marlow concludes:

> The conquest of the earth, which mostly means the taking it away from those who have a different complexion or slightly flatter noses than ourselves, is not a pretty thing when you look into it too much. What redeems it is the idea only. An idea at the back of it; not a sentimental pretence but an idea; and an unselfish belief in the idea – something you can set up, and bow down before, and offer a sacrifice to.   (50–1)

This seemingly contradictory statement forms one of the critical cruxes of the story. If the "conquest of the earth . . . is not a pretty thing when you look into it too much," then can it really be redeemed? Does Marlow accept colonialism, reject colonialism, or reject continental colonialism but accept British colonialism because of its "devotion to efficiency" and "unselfish belief in the idea"? An answer to this question becomes crucial in determining how one interprets "Heart of Darkness." Before answering this question, though, one must first determine what this "unselfish belief in the idea" is. Based upon what occurs later in the story, it seems that this "idea" is the idealistic goal of improving the non-Western world through the dissemination of Western culture, society, education, technology, and religion. Given Marlow's treatment of the colonial endeavor, as he experiences it in Africa, we can only conclude that he is highly critical of it. The more subtle nuances of this conclusion, though, are less clear. Despite Marlow's withering critique of colonialism, it remains unclear whether colonialism in general is under attack or only continental colonialism – particularly Belgian colonialism. In other words, by insisting that colonialism can be redeemed, Marlow leaves open the possibility that he exempts the British from his otherwise unrelenting indictment.

Leaving this question aside, however, what remains is a clear criticism of Western civilization as Marlow encounters it in Africa. The whole colonial endeavor, at least as it was represented at the time, consisted of an uneasy marriage between commercial colonial trade and an altruistic attempt to improve African life, as Kurtz is quoted as saying: "Each station should be like a beacon on the road towards better things, a centre for trade of course, but also for humanizing, improving, instructing" (91). Even if one grants the Eurocentric assumption that the non-Western world needed improving, the difficulty of marrying such incompatible motivations as economics and education seems to have proven to be beyond the abilities of even the most sincere colonizers. Invariably, the colonial endeavor ultimately became one of exploitation, and this exploitation becomes prominent in "Heart of Darkness." The public perception of colonial activities was one of paternalism, as Marlow's aunt demonstrates when she talks of Marlow's "weaning those ignorant millions from their horrid ways" (59). Marlow discovers, though, that the reality of the colonial experience in Africa is anything but "humanizing, improving, instructing." Marlow's fireman best exemplifies this problem:

> He was an improved specimen; he could fire up a vertical boiler . . . A few months of training had done for that really fine chap. He squinted at the steam-gauge and at the water-gauge with an evident effort of intrepidity – and he had filed teeth, too, the poor devil, and the wool of his pate shaved into queer patterns, and three ornamental scars on each of his cheeks . . . He was useful because he had been instructed; and what he knew was this – that should the water in that transparent thing disappear, the evil spirit inside the boiler would get angry through the greatness of his thirst, and take a terrible vengeance. So he sweated and fired up and watched the glass fearfully.   (97–8)

Clearly, the fireman's education is merely an expedient one for the colonial officials. They make no real attempt to "improve" him. They simply play upon his own beliefs and replace them with similar ones, and so Marlow refers to "the philanthropic pretence of the whole concern" (78). The company is only interested in cheap labor, not in educating the Africans about Western values and beliefs.

Further questioning of colonialism appears in the role of Western civilization in Africa. From the moment Marlow steps ashore in Africa, Western civilization appears to be absurd, out of place, or detrimental. Whether it be the "objectless blasting" (64), the chief accountant's attire (67–8), or the grove of death (66–7), Western civilization does not improve Africa or the Africans, and this initial representation only strengthens as the story progresses. If Western civilization is grounded in absolute truth (as most Westerners assumed), then it should thrive wherever disseminated. That it does not thrive in Africa calls into question any absolute quality. Furthermore, Marlow sees that not only does Western civilization not benefit the Africans, it does not benefit the Europeans either. Consistently, he observes that Western values and morals have little or no play in the lives of the Europeans working in the Congo. Instead, Marlow finds "a flabby, pretending, weak-eyed devil of a rapacious and pitiless folly" (65). Far from observing a "devotion to efficiency" (50) or centers "for humanizing, improving, instructing" (91), the Europeans seem generally devoid of Western values. On several occasions, one of the Europeans observes that Western morality does not come into play in Africa, as when the uncle of the Central Station manager says, "Anything – anything can be done in this country" (91). Marlow recognizes this dearth of morality and notes that without external restraints in the form of public opinion and law enforcement the Europeans do whatever they want. They have no "inborn strength" (97) to fight unchecked desires. As a result, the Europeans appear more savage than the Africans, whom the Europeans consider savages. Marlow underscores this point in the incident with the cannibals. In this scene, Marlow shows the cannibals first to be more rational than their European employers and second to be more moral. During the concern over a possible attack, the head cannibal says to Marlow, "Catch 'im . . . Give 'im to us." Marlow replies, "To you, eh? What would you do with them?" to which the cannibal replies, "Eat 'im!" (103). Marlow then continues:

> I would no doubt have been properly horrified, had it not occurred to
> me that he and his chaps must be very hungry: that they must have been
> growing increasingly hungry for at least this month past . . . and of
> course, as long as there was a piece of paper written over in accordance
> with some farcical law or other made down the river, it didn't enter
> anybody's head to trouble how they would live . . . they had given them

every week three pieces of brass wire, each about nine inches long; and the theory was they were to buy their provisions with that currency in river-side villages. You can see how *that* worked. There were either no villages, or the people were hostile . . . So, unless they swallowed the wire itself, or made loops of it to snare the fishes with, I don't see what good their extravagant salary could be to them. I must say it was paid with a regularity worthy of a large and honourable trading company.

(103–4)

Not only does this incident reveal the absurdity of Western civilization in an African setting (since the Western economic system makes no sense here), but it also shows the cannibals to be more rational than the Europeans. Marlow's point becomes even more emphatic because Europeans considered cannibalism to be the most savage behavior and the furthest removed from civilized behavior. That the cannibals act more rationally than the Europeans makes Conrad's comment on Western civilization that much more telling. Conrad does not stop there, though. Shortly after the above exchange, Marlow very reasonably wonders:

Why in the name of all the gnawing devils of hunger they didn't go for us – they were thirty to five – and have a good tuck-in for once, amazes me now when I think of it. They were big powerful men, with not much capacity to weigh the consequences, with courage, with strength . . . And I saw that something restraining, one of those human secrets that baffle probability, had come into play there . . . Restraint! What possible restraint? Was it superstition, disgust, patience, fear – or some kind of primitive honour? No fear can stand up to hunger, no patience can wear it out, disgust simply does not exist where hunger is; and as to superstition, beliefs, and what you may call principles, they are less than chaff in a breeze. Don't you know the devilry of lingering starvation, its exasperating torment, its black thoughts, its sombre and brooding ferocity? Well, I do. It takes a man all his inborn strength to fight hunger properly. It's really easier to face bereavement, dishonour, and the perdition of one's soul – than this kind of prolonged hunger. Sad, but true. And these chaps, too, had no earthly reason for any kind of scruple. Restraint! I would just as soon have expected restraint from a hyena prowling amongst the corpses of a battlefield.   (104–5)

Ironically, the restraint that the cannibals exhibit appears to be the only example of restraint in the story. The Europeans, who are supposed to be civilized, consistently lack any restraint except when confronted with external checks. In this case, the cannibals have no external restraints upon them, and yet they exhibit an internal restraint. Again, the fact that cannibals, whom the

Europeans thought were the most savage of beings, act the most civilized of any of the human beings Marlow encounters emphasizes the utter savagery at the heart of the Europeans when removed from the external restraints of Western civilization.

Experiences like this one, along with the general disorder, waste, and degeneration among the images of Western civilization, serve to erode Marlow's confidence in an orderly and absolute foundation for Western civilization. This erosion culminates in Marlow's experience with Kurtz and the Central Station manager. Kurtz is presented as the high point of Western civilization. Marlow is careful to note that "all Europe contributed to the making of Kurtz" (117), and that Kurtz is "a prodigy," "an emissary of pity, and science, and progress" (79), and a "universal genius" (83). He is one of "the gang of virtue" (79), going out into the African wilderness "equipped with moral ideas" (88) and with the purpose of disseminating Western values. Something goes wrong along the way, though. Removed from the external restraints of Western civilization, Kurtz has no internal restraint to keep him from doing whatever he pleases. The result is that rather than exerting "a power for good practically unbounded" (118), Kurtz concludes by presiding "at certain midnight dances ending with unspeakable rites, which . . . were offered up to him" (118). Far from being an "august Benevolence" (118), he ends up raiding the countryside in quest of more ivory. Marlow clearly disapproves of Kurtz, so it comes as some surprise that Marlow sides with him. It is important to remember, though, that in siding with Kurtz, Marlow is simply choosing one "nightmare" (138) over another. Kurtz represents good intentions gone terribly wrong. He had begun as a moral being with benevolent intentions but ultimately could not maintain his ideals once invested with absolute power. In the end, nothing was at the back of Kurtz – no solid foundation, as Marlow says, "He had kicked himself loose of the earth" (144).

The Central Station manager, however, is another case entirely. He commits none of Kurtz's evil acts and thoroughly disapproves of Kurtz and Kurtz's methods for collecting ivory. Yet, Marlow sides with Kurtz. Marlow does so, though, because of what the Central Station manager represents. In a telling conversation between the two, the manager remarks, "But there is no disguising the fact, Mr. Kurtz has done more harm than good to the Company. He did not see the time was not ripe for vigorous action . . . The district is closed to us for a time. Deplorable! Upon the whole, the trade will suffer . . . Look how precarious the position is – and why? Because the method is unsound" (137). Marlow comments concerning this conversation, "It seemed to me I had never breathed an atmosphere so vile, and I turned mentally to Kurtz for relief – positively for relief" (138). The relief Marlow seeks is in the world of morality and immorality that Kurtz represents. In contrast, the manager represents a world of amorality. This world of amorality had been evident for some time in the story. The most glaring example of it appears early in the story in the chief accountant's attitude toward an invalided agent and the African workers. He says of the agent, "The groans of this sick person distract my attention. And without that it is extremely difficult to guard against clerical errors in this climate" (69). Similarly, he remarks of the noise the Africans make, "When one has got to make correct entries, one comes to hate those savages – hate them to the death" (70). The tone of the Central Station manager's comments resembles that of the chief accountant. What Marlow refers to as Kurtz's raiding the country (128) the manager calls "vigorous action" (137), and the manager's objection to Kurtz's actions is not a moral objection but rather an economic one. He is unconcerned with the immorality of Kurtz's actions. Instead, he recognizes that because of Kurtz's methods trade in the area will suffer in the long run. For Marlow, the Central Station manager and so many of the other Europeans associated with the company appear outside morality. They are neither moral nor immoral but rather amoral, concerned only with the economics of the colonial endeavor – divorced from any altruistic feeling. In fact, they scoff at such ideas (e.g., 79, 91). Kurtz is wholly immoral, but his is the story of good morals gone bad. In contrast, the Central Station manager and almost every other European that Marlow encounters in Africa has neither moral nor immoral intentions. Consequently, they seem inhuman and utterly destroy any confidence Marlow might have had concerning the altruism of colonialism.

As a result of his experience in the African wilderness, Marlow's confidence in Western civilization and in any transcendental truths disappears, so much so that he concludes, "Droll thing life is – that mysterious arrangement of merciless logic for a futile purpose. The most you can hope from it is some knowledge of yourself – that comes too late – a crop of unextinguishable regrets" (150). Marlow has witnessed the stripping away of his civilized values and views, and he discovers that nothing lies beneath. Knowledge of this crucial truth is also exactly what the Europeans lack. Only Kurtz seems to recognize fully the naked truth concerning himself and his ideals when he sums up, "The horror! The horror!" (149). The rest of the Europeans in Africa remain oblivious to the things that Marlow learns. Nor do they seem to care to investigate such issues. When Marlow returns to Europe, he finds it no different:

> I found myself back in the sepulchral city resenting the sight of people hurrying through the streets to filch a little money from each other, to

devour their infamous cookery, to gulp their unwholesome beer, to dream their insignificant and silly dreams. They trespassed upon my thoughts. They were intruders whose knowledge of life was to me an irritating pretence, because I felt so sure they could not possibly know the things I knew. Their bearing, which was simply the bearing of commonplace individuals going about their business in the assurance of perfect safety, was offensive to me like the outrageous flauntings of folly in the face of a danger it is unable to comprehend.   (152)

Marlow sees these people as deluded and criticizes them because they do not know what he knows: that the truths of Western civilization are facades that hide an empty universe and that human existence has no ultimate meaning. While Marlow thinks that one should see the world as it is, at the same time he also wishes to keep such a bleak view at bay. As occurs so often with the characters in Conrad's works, Marlow seeks shelter from such withering knowledge. For him, this shelter seems to exist in the idealistic world of the Intended. Marlow's lie to the Intended has been the subject of some speculation. Clearly, he wishes to protect her and to spare her feelings, but Marlow also wants to protect himself. That his lie is significant is clear from his earlier comment: "You know I hate, detest, and can't bear a lie" (82), and yet he lies to the Intended about Kurtz's last words. Earlier, Marlow had remarked, "We must help them [women] to stay in that beautiful world of their own, lest ours gets worse" (115), and when he comments on his lie he says, "I could not tell her. It would have been too dark – too dark altogether . . ." (162). By telling the Intended the truth, Marlow would have shattered the pristine world that she and other women inhabit. By lying to her, he preserves that world of ideals, which acts as a psychological refuge for Marlow from the bleak truths he has discovered outside it.

The story ends with a picture of the Thames that resembles the darkness of the Congo river far more than it does the origins of "the sacred fire" (47) of civilization. Marlow's journey, as well as that of his listeners, has been one of discovery – discovery of the nature of his self, his existence, and his world.

"The End of the Tether" is another tale that investigates moral and psychological dilemmas. Captain Whalley has an almost obsessive devotion to his daughter Ivy and intends to provide for her. After a lifetime of hard work and honorable actions, Captain Whalley loses most of his savings in a bank failure. He sells his ship and sends the money to Ivy so that she can open a boarding house. Whalley then signs on as captain of the *Sephora*, which is owned by Mr. Massy, a notoriously shady individual. Whalley invests his last £500 in the *Sephora* with the understanding that after he has served a three-year term as captain his investment will be paid back to him. During his time as captain, Whalley's eyesight begins to fail drastically, but he continues in his position in order to receive back his investment (which would have been delayed if he had left his position early). After they nearly run aground near Batu Beru, Mr. Sterne, the mate, suspects a problem with the captain's eyesight and tells Massy. Massy does nothing because he hopes to take advantage of the situation. Having already lost Whalley's investment gambling, Massy hangs pieces of iron near the compass to throw the ship off course and sink it in order to collect the insurance money. Unable to see the reef and deceived by the compass, Whalley runs the ship aground. Whalley discovers Massy's trick, but he chooses to go down with the ship.

Most commentators have viewed "The End of the Tether" as one of Conrad's lesser works, but during the course of the story Conrad investigates several important issues in unique ways. For example, Whalley's plight is a stark reminder of the frailty of human existence. In one blow, Whalley's world is unalterably changed; and the bank failure demonstrates that human beings have little control over their existence and are ultimately at the mercy of the whims of fate. Conrad further emphasizes this idea through the gambling motif that runs throughout the story. Both in Massy's gambling with money and in Whalley's gambling with the ship's safety, chance remains in the forefront of the action of the story.

Conrad also investigates the relationship between loyalty to a social code and loyalty to an individual. Conrad considers this conflict in a number of his works, although he never seems to come to a definitive conclusion. In such works as *Lord Jim*, *Nostromo*, and *Under Western Eyes*, Conrad seems to privilege loyalty to an individual. In *Nostromo*, for instance, the narrator comments: "A man haunted by a fixed idea is insane. He is dangerous even if that idea is an idea of justice; for may he not bring the heaven down pitilessly upon a loved head?" (379). In "The End of the Tether," however, despite obvious sympathy for Whalley's plight, Conrad clearly condemns Whalley's actions. By signing on to work for Massy, and especially by continuing in his position once his eyesight had deteriorated, Whalley compromises his honor and principles, which had been the basis for his life. He exchanged his principles for his daughter, and he fully recognizes the import of this transaction: "He had nothing of his own – even his past of honour, of truth, of just pride, was gone. All his spotless life had fallen into the abyss" (319). Although Whalley remains loyal to his daughter, he risks the lives of his crew and the property of Massy. In this case, the price Whalley pays in sacrificing the social code is too high, and Conrad further emphasizes his disapproval by portraying Ivy as unworthy of Whalley's sacrifice. "The End of the Tether" is unique because it represents one of the very few times when Conrad sides with an idea over a human relationship.

Lord Jim

Lord Jim deals with the problems of lost honor, Romantic idealism, and the conflict between human relations and ideas. It is a novel that chronicles the experiences of a seaman named Jim. At an early age, Jim wants to go to sea to experience the adventures he reads about in popular literature. He goes to a training school and later enters the British Merchant Marine service. Shortly thereafter, he accepts a position as second mate aboard the *Patna*. The ship has been engaged to carry some 800 Muslims on a pilgrimage to Mecca. One night, the *Patna* collides with some object (perhaps a partially sunken wreck) and begins taking on water. Jim goes below and sees that nothing can be done, given the vessel's poor condition. He goes back on deck and initially waits for the inevitable end. In the meantime, the other officers busy themselves trying to flee the ship. They lower one of the lifeboats and jump in. At the last moment, Jim also jumps in. Later, they are rescued, believing that the ship has sunk. Ironically, defying all probability, the ship does not sink, and when the officers reach port news of the *Patna*'s rescue has already arrived. The other officers abscond, but Jim stays to stand trial. His certificate is revoked and for the next several years he wanders about various seaports throughout the East drifting from one job to another, each time leaving when his shameful past arises. In the end, Marlow, who has befriended Jim, arranges through Stein to have Jim sent out to be in charge of an obscure trading post in Patusan. Jim arrives and leads one of the local villages against their oppressor, Sherif Ali, and succeeds in routing his forces. In so doing, Jim becomes a hero to the people and achieves an almost legendary status. Jim continues in this position until a renegade named Gentleman Brown comes up the river in search of food and spoils. Jim is away when Brown arrives, and when he returns, Brown and his men have been repulsed and are under siege. Jim meets with Brown, and Brown convinces Jim either to fight it out or to let Brown and his men leave unmolested. Brown intuitively plays upon Jim's continuing feelings of guilt over the *Patna* incident, and Jim convinces the people of Patusan to allow Brown to leave. Unknown to Jim, Cornelius (whom Jim had been sent to replace as Stein's agent) shows Brown another way out, and Brown takes the opportunity to ambush a group of Patusani warriors during their retreat. The son of Doramin, the leader of Patusan, is killed in the ambush, and Jim, who had pledged his life on his decision, leaves his common-law wife, Jewel, and goes to Doramin, who shoots and kills him.

This summary of the book's plot, though, is far more direct than the narrative itself. Although Conrad had previously experimented with innovations in narrative technique, such as multiple narrators and achronological narration, these innovations first appear fully developed in *Lord Jim*. Conrad employed multiple narrators in "Heart of Darkness," for example, but his use there was much more tentative and much more limited. In *Lord Jim*, however, this technique blossoms into a powerful and effective means of conveying the novel's difficult and crucial concerns. Jim's story comes from various narrative sources, among them an omniscient narrator, Marlow, Gentleman Brown, Ëgstrom, Tamb' Itam, Stein, Jewel, and Jim himself. All of these narrators (and others as well) tell a part of Jim's story, but more particularly they represent a perspective on Jim's story. In other words, besides providing information, they also provide a point of view on that information. As a result, the story of Jim is not a sum of parts adding up to a relative whole but rather a sum of perspectives adding up to an aggregate. Of course, such a narrative technique represents reality, since it resembles the way any story is usually a collection assembled from various sources. More than this, though, by employing multiple narrators, Conrad emphasizes the uncertainty of the final aggregate, suggesting that since all information is filtered through a human consciousness, knowledge can never be certain.

Tied to Conrad's use of multiple narrators is his use of achronological narration. Where "Heart of Darkness" was subtly achronological, *Lord Jim* is bewilderingly so. Particularly during the chapters narrated by the omniscient narrator but even after Marlow takes up the narrative, most readers coming to the novel for the first time find it difficult to follow the sequence of events. The achronology occurs in part because of multiple narrators telling different parts of the story non-consecutively, and it also occurs because Marlow's listeners know parts of the story that the reader does not. Conrad's reasons, however, for employing an achronological narrative are another matter. Like multiple narrators, Conrad represents the way one usually learns of an event, that is by learning segments of it and only in the very rarest instances encountering those segments in chronological order. More important, though, by using this methodology, Conrad can represent in narrative form the issues raised in the novel. In other words, the confusion of the narrative technique mirrors the confusion of the moral issues considered. Furthermore, like multiple narrators, fracturing the narrative sequence represents the fractured facts that Marlow must piece together and that can lead to only a tentative knowledge of what happened. Again, the narrative methodology emphasizes the subjectivity of knowledge and the impossibility of knowing anything for certain.

The issue of Romanticism is one of the most important in *Lord Jim*. As Stein had ascertained, Jim is indeed a Romantic, and Jim's Romanticism is one of Conrad's primary points of investigation. After abandoning the *Patna*, Jim's reaction is similar to what he had done after he failed aboard the training ship as a youth. Rather than recognizing his failure, he sees himself as a victim of circumstances that conspired to thwart him. As a result, he continues to see himself as a heroic figure and believes that if he can just get another chance he can prove himself to be a hero. The difficulty with this view is that he does not realize that there are no second chances. The maritime community requires absolute fidelity to a "fixed standard of conduct" (50). This standard of conduct does not allow for failure.

Jim's trouble, however, goes beyond himself. Throughout the novel, Marlow refers to Jim as "one of us." This refrain becomes a crucial issue in the book, and Jim's individual concerns become the community's collective concerns. Jim reminds the members of the community, and Marlow in particular, of themselves when they were young, and thus they see themselves in Jim's failure. Marlow follows Jim's career and offers help where he can, out of friendship and compassion to be sure, but also out of self interest. Marlow hopes to find some excuse for Jim's failure because he sees himself in Jim. Marlow also hopes for an explanation so that he can again have full confidence in the maritime code because what becomes clear to Marlow is that in the same circumstances anyone might have failed as Jim had failed; hence the code's unbending demands become suspect.

Besides the code itself, Conrad further questions the basis for its code in Western ideals. If the code fails to hold up against scrutiny, then Western ideals may come into question as well. Conrad's criticism, however, goes even deeper than simply criticizing Romantic cultural ideals and the maritime code of conduct. He also criticizes Western cultural ideals in general. In other words, ultimately, the origin of both Romantic ideals and the ideals of the maritime code of conduct is a group of Western cultural values that require a perfection that is illusory. The story of Brierly emphasizes Conrad's skepticism concerning Western ideals. Conrad clearly sets up Brierly as an example of the best that the maritime service can offer:

> He had never in his life made a mistake, never had an accident, never a mishap, never a check in his steady rise, and he seemed to be one of those lucky fellows who know nothing of indecision, much less of self-mistrust. At thirty-two he had one of the best commands going in the

> Eastern trade . . . He had saved lives at sea, had rescued ships in distress, had a gold chronometer presented to him by the underwriters, and a pair of binoculars with a suitable inscription from some foreign Government, in commemoration of these services.   (57)

Everyone seems to agree; even those who dislike Brierly recognize his abilities, and yet Marlow is careful to point out that Brierly's suicide results directly from his involvement with Jim's case. Marlow remarks that during Jim's trial Brierly "was probably holding silent inquiry into his own case. The verdict must have been of unmitigated guilt" (58), and later Marlow says that "poor Brierly must have been thinking of himself" (66) when he talked to Marlow of Jim's case. In the end, we cannot fully understand the reason for Brierly's suicide, but he is clearly troubled by Jim's case, and whether he seeks to conceal a previous failure or perhaps is simply unwilling to allow himself the possibility of Jim's sort of failure, the result is essentially the same: he seems to recognize, as had Marlow, that given the right set of circumstances perhaps anyone could fail. Thus, with the case of Brierly, Conrad again calls into question the code itself, suggesting that if no one can live up to the code's standards, then the standards themselves are faulty. Such is the unavoidable conclusion regarding the ideals of the code, and, as with the Romantic ideals that so govern Jim's existence, the ultimate source of the code's ideals is Western civilization itself. Jim's downfall, as was true of Brierly's, results from the idealistic code to which he adheres, and his inability to abandon the code when he enters Patusan leaves him susceptible to Gentleman Brown's manipulation. In this way, Western civilization itself comes into question in *Lord Jim*.

Marlow's insistence that Jim is "one of us" is also significant in determining the breadth of the implications of Jim's behavior and failings. Conrad is consistently vague about the reference of Marlow's statement "one of us." Does Marlow refer to human beings in general, only to Westerners, to members of the maritime community, to the officers of the maritime community, to the gentleman class of the Western world – or to all of them? One thing is clear, though: Jim's failure is not an individual failure but rather a community failure. As a result, the other characters and even Conrad's readers must ask themselves the question that Jim asks Marlow: "what would you have done?" (92).

Conrad further questions the ideals that appear in the novel by considering the end result of following those ideals. The ideals consistently appear at odds with human relations. The conflict most clearly appears in the conclusion to the novel, in which Marlow lays out the alternatives when he says, "He goes away from a living woman to celebrate his pitiless wedding with a shadowy ideal of conduct" (416). Marlow can only question the merit of choosing an idea – particularly one that has been shown to be illusory – over the human relationship that existed between Jim and Jewel.

Nevertheless, as so often in his best works, Conrad does not leave things so easily resolved. Conrad's criticism of Jim's choice is clear, but Jim's plight is not. The communion between Jim and Jewel is one example of the idea of community that is so important in *Lord Jim*. Marlow's constant refrain that Jim is "one of us" along with Jim's relationship to the maritime fraternity keeps the issue of community prominent among the novel's concerns. Jim spends the entire novel trying to make his way back into the maritime community. Once he jumps from the *Patna*, Jim seems forever to forfeit his membership and finds himself alone, an outcast from the community. After his jump, all of Jim's choices are meant to demonstrate that he belongs. Jim's plight becomes the plight of all human beings in their desire to belong. All are isolated in the modern world, and any communal bonds one acquires are both tentative and transitory, and yet without such bonds, one can only despair, as Jim does. Jim sees his choice to meet Doramin rather than staying with Jewel as his reinstatement in the community from which he had been cast out. In his mind, he is once again "one of us." Consequently, Jim's dilemma is such that he must choose not just between a communal bond with Jewel or upholding an ideal but also between a bond with Jewel or a bond with his community. He cannot maintain both bonds. Marlow is critical of Jim's choice, but he himself is unwilling to relinquish his ties to the community, even though he recognizes that it rests not upon a transcendent foundation but merely upon the common consent of its members. Such is the human desire to belong.

Similarly, even Conrad's critique of the ideals upon which Jim's choice is based is not clear. Conrad certainly criticizes Western ideals, but at the same time, he refuses to dismiss them entirely. This conflict appears most prominently in Stein's comments on Jim's Romanticism: "And that is very bad – very bad . . . Very good, too" (216). Jim's Romanticism is bad for all of the reasons listed above (and for others as well). In particular, as Stein suggests, Romanticism is bad because it is never content with the status quo. It always looks to go beyond the limits imposed upon it. Thus, it represents an ultimate impossibility: perfection. At the same time, though, Romantic idealism is good, according to Stein, and it is good for exactly the same reasons that it is bad, because it espouses never being satisfied with one's condition, constantly striving for improvement, and always seeking to go beyond limitations. This ambiguity results in what appears so often in Conrad – a recognition of the illusory nature of Western ideals and the absolutes upon which it is based, but at the same time a recognition of certain qualities in human beings (the constant striving for betterment, the desire to improve one's circumstances, the wish to push beyond limitations) that Conrad believed make human beings human. The result of these conflicted views is an uncertainty that marks Conrad's works in general and marks Conrad's view of the world as a whole.

"Typhoon" and Other Stories

"Typhoon" introduces the reader to Captain MacWhirr, an unimaginative man, who commands the *Nan-Shan* and is taking two hundred Chinese workers back to China. During the course of the journey, they encounter bad weather, but rather than trying to maneuver around the storm MacWhirr takes the ship straight into it. To make matters worse, the passengers' belongings become hopelessly mixed together, and the Chinese below deck begin rioting and fighting over their money, which has been thrown about everywhere. The crew finally restores order, and somehow the ship makes it through the storm. With everything in a shambles below, MacWhirr decides that the only fair thing to do is to gather up all of the lost money and divide it equally among the passengers, which he does.

Conrad's narrative technique in the story is unusual, as the information comes from a variety of sources, a third-person narrator, who relates more than one perspective, as well as letters by crew members. The result is similar to that in *Lord Jim*, for instance, although on a smaller scale. In other words, the reader sees the events narrated from several perspectives and recognizes the inherent inability to know anything with certainty since so much is determined by the source from which it comes.

"Typhoon" is a companion piece of sorts to *The Nigger of the "Narcissus."* Both stories deal with the effects of a storm on a ship's crew, and both also consider the relationship between the idea of community and human survival. "Typhoon" presents one of the more interesting characters in Conrad's canon: Captain MacWhirr. Initially, it would seem easy to dismiss him. Early on, MacWhirr is described as "having just enough imagination to carry him through each successive day, and no more, he was tranquilly sure of himself" (4). Later, Conrad notes:

> Captain MacWhirr had sailed over the surface of the oceans as some
> men go skimming over the years of existence to sink gently into a placid

> grave, ignorant of life to the last, without ever having been made to
> see all it may contain of perfidy, of violence, and of terror. There are
> on sea and land such men thus fortunate – or thus disdained by destiny
> or by the sea.   (19)

MacWhirr's very obliviousness, however, is exactly what allows him and his crew to survive the typhoon. He is supremely unimaginative, and as such is a counterexample to Jim in *Lord Jim*, whose imagination causes him to fail when confronted with a crisis. Furthermore, MacWhirr's stolidity serves as a comfort and strength to his crew, providing the men with an example of decisiveness and immovability in facing the storm. He also represents an individual who can focus solely on the task at hand, sheltered from larger issues. MacWhirr's ability is both "fortunate" and "disdained." Throughout his writings, Conrad demonstrates the need to be free from illusions about the nature of the world, that no transcendence exists to provide meaning in the universe or in human existence. At the same time, Conrad also demonstrates the need to be able to shelter oneself from such knowledge; otherwise, one can only despair. MacWhirr, although disdained for his obtuseness, is nevertheless fortunate in that he never has to struggle with the more difficult issues surrounding human existence. This characteristic also serves MacWhirr well when dealing with the distribution of the Chinese passengers' property. His decision to divide it evenly among them is surprisingly successful and causes Jukes, the chief mate, to conclude, "I think that he got out of it very well for such a stupid man" (102).

Thus the primary purpose of the story is not so much to relate an exciting event – the climax of which Conrad entirely skips – but rather to investigate the psychological and sociological reactions of the men in crisis. The crew members must maintain community through their mutual cooperation in order to keep the ship afloat during the storm. At the same time, though, Conrad demonstrates the ultimate isolation of human beings from one another. The typhoon accentuates this state, and as a result a tension exists in the story between community and isolation. Thus, "Typhoon" becomes a metaphor for human existence in general. For Conrad, human beings find themselves in an indifferent universe in which danger and death are always just around the corner. In addition, as has been shown in Conrad's other works, human existence itself is a paradox in that one requires communal relationships, but at the same time all communal ties are at best tenuous, dependent solely upon the mutual consent of a community's members. Hence, like the men on the *Nan-Shan*, human beings seek to connect with others, but in the end they are ultimately alone.

"To-morrow" is the story of retired Captain Hagberd, who continually puts off everything until "to-morrow" when his long-lost son, Harry, will return. Hagberd befriends his neighbor, Bessie Carvil, whose father tyrannizes over her, and says that his son will marry her when he returns. The great irony is that when his son does return the Captain fails to recognize him, and when the son learns of his father's misplaced intention of marrying him to Bessie, he leaves again. The story ends with Hagberd continuing to express his faith in "to-morrow."

The captain's delusional obsession is another of Conrad's psychological investigations into the way human beings cope with the uncertainty of human existence. On the one hand, Hagberd's delusion leaves him perpetually out of touch with reality, but on the other hand, it provides an anchor of hope that allows him to deal with the uncertainty of life and the future. Hagberd's delusion stands in stark contrast to Bessie's situation. While Hagberd can retreat into his delusion when Harry leaves once again, Bessie knows that Harry will not return again to his father or to her, and she is thus forced to back into her hellish existence. The story is also noteworthy because of the sympathetic treatment of Bessie's situation. Conrad delineates the bleak position in which most unmarried women found themselves at that time. With employment opportunities both scarce and meager, unmarried women were often left dependent upon relatives. Marrying Harry (or anyone else) is her only opportunity to escape from her domineering father, but the story makes clear that, unlike Harry, Bessie cannot escape her father.

"Amy Foster" has long been viewed as a story with autobiographical overtones. A Pole, Yanko Goorall, seeks to emigrate to America. When the ship he is aboard sinks, he is cast ashore in an isolated part of Kent and finds himself an outcast in the community, unable to communicate fully or integrate into society. Only Amy Foster befriends him, and they eventually marry. Cultural differences, however, again arise, this time between Goorall and his wife. A simple woman, she is troubled by Goorall's foreign habits, particularly his trying to teach their baby Polish. One night Goorall falls ill and frightens Amy when in his delirium he calls for water in Polish. Amy flees, leaving Goorall to die alone.

To be sure, Conrad must have had his own situation in mind as a Pole. Conrad himself must have often felt isolated, usually the only Pole in his community and married to an English woman who, like Amy Foster, was often troubled by Conrad's foreign behavior. Nevertheless, to suggest that the story is solely an autobiographical allegory would be oversimplifying. Instead, "Amy Foster" investigates the general question of the interaction between different cultures and shows that misunderstandings and difficulties abound when cultures collide. In a particularly interesting way, Conrad looks at this question from the other side of British culture. Rather than considering how the English (or other Europeans) interact with non-Western cultures, as Conrad does so often in his early fiction, "Amy Foster" considers the plight of the outsider within England. The result is a different kind of critique of British interaction with outsiders. In other words, Conrad demonstrates that the difficulties that arise when Western and non-Western cultures interact result not simply from differing settings and societies but rather from a general human inability to accept difference in others. In the process, Conrad uncovers the fear, suspicion, and biases that exist toward outsiders, as Goorall is systematically isolated from the community. "Amy Foster" is also strongly concerned with the nature of the relationship between the individual and society. Goorall's plight demonstrates the need for individuals to become part of a community and the ultimate despair that results from the inability to do so. The only character who seems to accept Goorall is Amy Foster. Even she, though, cannot fully accept him in the end, and when she deserts him during his illness, the isolation proves to be too much for Goorall to bear, and he dies of "heart-failure" (141).

"Falk: A Reminiscence" is a story of the collision of two radically different value systems: the Western system and the survivalist system. The story begins with a young captain going to visit a friend Hermann and his family. Later, when the young captain is ready to leave port, he cannot get Falk, the owner of the only tug-boat, to tow him out to sea. Falk even goes so far as to make sure that the young captain cannot hire any other pilot for the job. Mystified, the young captain happens to run into Falk one day and discovers that Falk has mistaken the young captain for a suitor to Hermann's niece, whom Falk wishes to marry. The young captain assures Falk that he is no suitor and even offers to act as Falk's advocate. Falk then tells the young captain of a significant experience in his past. Before the events in the story, Falk had been on a ship adrift for a long time. The food supply was eventually exhausted, and at one point the ship's carpenter tries to shoot Falk, with the idea of eating Falk's corpse. The carpenter's shot misses, and Falk shoots the carpenter dead. The remaining crew members then eat the carpenter's body. When the crew are finally rescued, besides Falk, only three others remain, and those three eventually die. Falk alone survives the catastrophe. When Mr. and Mrs. Hermann learn of Falk's past, they are horrified and want nothing to do with him. Hermann's niece, however, pities Falk and determines to marry him.

The significance of these events lies in the conflict that arises between the Western taboo against cannibalism and the exigencies that Falk's situation demands. Falk is determined to survive at all costs and discards the cultural taboo. The result of this conflict between value systems is such that Hermann's Western values come into question, and Falk's actions appear to be much more reasonable given the circumstances. Had Falk held to his Western values, he would have perished. In addition to this conflict of values, Falk's experience provides a strong reminder concerning the kind of world in which human beings exist. Far from being the place of safety and comfort that the Western world provides, the thin wall of civilization is all that separates one from the possibility of tragedy or death. In the story, Conrad further investigates the relationship between human beings and the world around them in the narrator's experience with Falk. As also happens later to Razumov in *Under Western Eyes*, the narrator finds himself in a world that makes no sense. He cannot sail out of port without Falk's help, and Falk inexplicably refuses to help him and ensures that no one else can help him either. As Razumov finds himself helplessly enmeshed in Haldin's crime, or as D'Hubert in "The Duel" finds himself caught in a seemingly endless cycle of duels, so also does the narrator of "Falk" find himself caught in the middle of a dispute of which he has no knowledge. Not until the narrator discovers that Falk sees him as a rival can he extricate himself from the absurdist existence into which he stumbles. The implication of this situation is, of course, that the world is a place that makes no rational sense, a place in which human beings have little control over their existence and are ultimately subject to forces outside themselves.

Nostromo

Nostromo is the first of Conrad's openly political novels. It is clearly Conrad's most ambitious work, and many argue that it is his finest novel. During the course of the novel, Conrad does no less than create an imaginary South American country, complete with history, politics, international relations, and society. The sheer magnitude of such a creation is itself remarkable.

Charles Gould has been away at school and returns to Sulaco in the country of Costaguana intent on making a success of the defunct silver mine that had been given to Gould's father in repayment for forced loans to the government. With the financial backing of Holroyd, an American financier, Gould eventually makes the mine a success. For a short while, relative peace and prosperity reign until General Montero initiates a coup. Don Vincente Ribiera, president of Costaguana, is defeated and forced to flee the country. Fearful that six-months-worth of silver from the mine will fall into the hands of the Monterists, Gould arranges to have it spirited out of the country by boat. Martin Decoud and Nostromo are entrusted with the task, but on route, the boat collides with a rebel troopship and is forced to land on an isolated island, where Decoud and Nostromo hide the silver. Nostromo then swims back to Sulaco. Shortly after arriving, Dr. Monygham enlists Nostromo to ride to Cayta to bring back General Barrios to fight the Monterists, who have arrived in Sulaco in an attempt to secure the silver mine. Gould, however, has taken precautions to prevent such an event by leaving instructions that if it is attacked Don Pépé is to blow up the mine. Barrios arrives and defeats the Monterists and succeeds in bringing about a plan that Decoud had proposed that the geographically isolated Occidental province, of which Sulaco is a part, secede from the rest of Costaguana. Ironically, Decoud, left alone on the island for a number of days, grows depressed and assumes that all has failed. One morning he rows a little way offshore and shoots himself, falling into the water, weighed down by four silver ingots. Several years pass, and Sulaco has become a prosperous place. Gould and the mine are flourishing, and Nostromo owns his own ship and trading business. All appears well in Sulaco, except for the growing labor unrest. Also, Nostromo, having returned to the hidden silver, discovered Decoud and the four ingots missing. Everyone has assumed that the silver was lost after the collision, and Nostromo, who is afraid to reveal the silver's hiding place for fear that he would be accused of stealing the missing ingots, decides to take the ingots one by one and slowly grow rich. During this time, Giorgio Viola, who has been like a second father to Nostromo, has been placed in charge of the newly built lighthouse on the very island where the silver is hidden. One night, while Nostromo is going to retrieve more silver, Giorgio mistakes him for an intruder and shoots him. Nostromo dies shortly afterwards.

Nostromo is a darkly pessimistic novel that juxtaposes political issues with issues of human relationships, interweaving these throughout the course of the narrative. It is easily Conrad's longest and most complex novel, and it is a rare reader who upon first reading it can find his or her way through the labyrinth of plots, plethora of characters, and fragmented sequence of events without experiencing confusion. In fact, there may be points in the novel in which it is impossible fully to understand the events that are being related without first knowing details that do not come until later.

This narrative confusion serves two purposes. As he does elsewhere, Conrad attempts to render the way individuals usually approach an event new to them, that is by learning different pieces from different sources and typically encountering these sources achronologically. Unlike in "Heart of Darkness" and *Lord Jim*, in which Conrad employed multiple narrators whose information then filtered through the main narrator Marlow, *Nostromo* employs an omniscient narrator, who relates the characters' differing perspectives. As was true of the omniscient narrator of the first few chapters of *Lord Jim*, this omniscient narrator is certainly a very unusual one, who withholds information from the reader and who relates events in an achronological fashion. In *Nostromo*, Conrad achieves the same ends with his narrative methodology as he did in *Lord Jim* and "Heart of Darkness." The differing views of events, even though related by a single omniscient narrator, still demonstrate the relativity and subjectivity of knowledge, and the achronological narrative technique similarly demonstrates the uncertainty of knowledge. At the same time, though, the multiple perspectives and fractured chronology that result in the novel's narrative confusion also mirror the moral and political confusion that so permeates the novel.

Throughout the novel, Conrad indicts politics on all levels. Consistently, he portrays the revolutionaries as self-serving, brutal, greedy, and power hungry. Despite their rhetoric, they are anything but altruistic. Conrad, however, is not much more positive toward the Ribiera government or Sulaco secessionist government at the end of the novel. The Ribiera government was ushered in through the influence of Gould and the mine, and although it appears to be better than its predecessors, that is not saying much since Costaguana's history has been one of consistent brutality, waste, greed, and stupidity. Even amongst the Ribiera government, corruption is rampant, and most of its positive qualities only appear so because they are set against the background of previous governments. As to the Sulaco government, it bears the marks of a European democracy and appears to be progressive in its thinking. However, the mine is at its heart, and it is founded upon material interests rather than upon thoughts of the common good. The government's inception and its primary purpose is to protect the interests of the mine – not the people. Some political peace and economic prosperity result, but they are not the main goal of the government. In this sense, the government exhibits a kind of inhumanity. Add to this the tenuous political peace, and the picture of Sulaco at the end of the novel is hardly as rosy as Captain Mitchell, for example, thinks it to be (489).

Linked to the political situation in Costaguana are Conrad's comments on imperialism, but rather than looking at imperialism in Africa or Southeast Asia, Conrad considers imperialism in the new world, particularly the way European and American imperialist policies affected Latin America. Much of the political instability, revolutionary activity, and economic turmoil result from the interference of Europe and America. Gould is of English descent; Decoud is of French descent; Holroyd is American. These individuals as well as others and various European and American business and government interests are a source of friction between the Costaguanans and the Blancos (the aristocrats of European descent). The Monteros' primary propaganda revolves around driving out European and American political and business interests in Costaguana. In short, Conrad sees the mess that Costaguana has become resulting largely from imperialist interference.

The source of imperialist activities in *Nostromo* is the silver. Conrad had considered naming the novel *The Silver of the Mine*, and such a title would have been appropriate since everything that occurs revolves around the silver. The silver is the object of Gould's enterprises, the goal of the revolutionaries, the primary underpinning of the country's economy, the practical support for the government, and the source of so much that happens in Costaguana. In short, the silver permeates the existence of every member of society, particularly those living in Sulaco and its surroundings. The great irony is that the country's greatest success at the end of the novel, its economic prosperity and stability, is also its greatest failure. Although Gould's father received the rights to the mine as repayment for loans, he was forced to pay royalties on the mine's potential. The strain and humiliation of this situation eventually kills Gould's father, who warns Charles not to return to Costaguana, but Charles ignores his father's warning and returns equipped with an engineering degree and financial backing. He then proceeds to take the mine, which his father thought to be a curse, and resurrect it, making it a prosperous and powerful force in the country. A further result of the mine's success lies in the political stability it provides. All of this ought to indicate an unmitigated success, particularly given the political and economic chaos and turmoil of so much of Costaguana's history. In one sense, the mine is certainly a great success – but in another sense it is an abject failure.

The cost of the mine's success is great. The short time of political peace during Ribiera's presidency eventually crumbles into chaos and revolution, the primary goal of the revolutionaries being to gain control of the mine. Without the mine as a prize, the Monteros might have been less inclined to overthrow Ribiera's government. Even more telling is the political atmosphere at the end of the novel, though. The Sulaco government contrasts with the typical political machinations that marred Costaguana's past. The region grows in prosperity and peace, and in Captain Mitchell's words, "It is a success," "the 'Treasure House of the World'" (489). Beneath this success, however, lies a smoldering danger. As Dr. Monygham prophesies, "There is no peace and no rest in the development of material interests . . . the time approaches when all that the Gould Concession stands for shall weigh as heavily upon the people as the barbarism, cruelty, and misrule of a few years back" (511). And the narrator says of Mrs. Gould, "She saw the San Tomé mountain hanging over the Campo, over the whole land, feared, hated, wealthy; more soulless than any tyrant, more pitiless and autocratic than the worst Government; ready to crush innumerable lives in the expansion of its greatness" (521). The developing labor unrest and the unavoidable control the mine exerts over the lives of all of those who live within Sulaco presage an ominous sequel to the events chronicled in *Nostromo*.

More troubling than the smoldering political unrest, though, is the mine's toll in human cost, as it destroys so many individuals either physically or spiritually. Charles and Emilia Gould, Nostromo, Gould's father, Decoud, Hirsch, the revolutionaries, the federalists, the counter-revolutionaries, the mine workers, and the politicians are all damaged in some way or other. The mine kills Gould's father, as well as Hirsch and the revolutionaries, federalists, counter-revolutionaries, and politicians who die during the Monterist revolt. Decoud's suicide can also be linked to the mine. The mine's most devastating effect, however, appears in the character changes that occur in so many individuals. Their lives are transformed from lives of peace and stability to lives of unrest and greed. Sotillo, the Monteros, and their followers attempt their revolt primarily because of the mine, and the mine workers and other laborers in Sulaco at the end of the novel also live lives of unrest because they want a greater part of the mine's profits. Charles Gould, Nostromo, and Emilia Gould, though, are those most affected by the mine.

Charles Gould begins with high ideals. He remarks, "What is wanted here is law, good faith, order, security. Any one can declaim about these things, but I pin my faith to material interests. Only let the material interests once get a firm footing, and they are bound to impose the conditions on which alone they can continue to exist" (84). He believes that if the mine can be made prosperous, political stability and economic prosperity will follow. As noted above, in many ways, Gould is correct, and the prosperity and success of the mine translate into peace and prosperity for Sulaco. In this sense, Gould is a great success – but at a great cost. The narrator notes that the "mine had got hold of Charles Gould with a grip as deadly as ever it had laid upon his father" (400) and that it "had insidiously corrupted his judgment" (364). In the process of making the mine a success, it becomes Gould's sole focus and ultimately becomes a barrier between him and his wife (239). Decoud writes to his sister that Emilia Gould "has discovered that he [Charles] lives for the mine rather than for her" (245). Eventually, she realizes that she "would never have him to herself. Never; not for one short hour altogether to herself" (521–2). Gould ends emotionally dead, always choosing the mine over Emilia.

Although Emilia Gould does not experience the same change of character that Charles does, she still experiences the devastating effects of the mine's influence. Emilia had joined Charles in his idealistic quest to make the mine a success, hoping that its economic prosperity would be a blessing to the region. She discovers instead that it becomes a curse, particularly to herself:

> The fate of the San Tomé mine was lying heavy upon her heart. It was a long time now since she had begun to fear it. It had been an idea. She had watched it with misgivings turning into a fetish, and now the fetish had grown into a monstrous and crushing weight. It was as if the inspiration of their early years had left her heart to turn into a wall of silver-bricks, erected by the silent work of evil spirits, between her and her husband. (221–2)

By the end of the novel, she thinks, "A terrible success for the last of the Goulds. The last! She hoped for a long, long time, that perhaps – But no! There were to be no more. An immense desolation, the dread of her own continued life, descended upon the first lady of Sulaco" (522). She loses not only her husband to the mine but also any hope she had for the comfort children might have brought, and is thus alone in the world.

The mine also destroys Nostromo. When we first meet him, he is at peace with himself and is universally respected and admired. Captain Mitchell refers to him as "invaluable . . . a perfectly incorruptible fellow" (127). Almost from the moment Nostromo is enlisted to keep the shipment of silver from the revolutionaries, however, he begins to change. He complains to Decoud and Monygham about his precarious position in protecting the silver, and after he begins to steal the silver he loses everything: "Nostromo had lost his peace; the genuineness of all his qualities was destroyed. He felt it himself, and often cursed the silver of San Tomé" (523). Nostromo no longer possesses those qualities that had made him who he was. Instead, he becomes obsessed with the silver:

> He could never shake off the treasure. His audacity, greater than that of other men, had welded that vein of silver into his life. And the feeling of fearful and ardent subjection, the feeling of his slavery – so irremediable and profound that often, in his thoughts, he compared himself to the legendary Gringos, neither dead nor alive, bound down to their conquest of unlawful wealth on Azuera – weighed heavily on the independent Captain Fidanza. (526–7)

Nostromo becomes the silver's "faithful and lifelong slave" (501). He recognizes what has happened to him and feels "the weight as of chains upon his limbs" (539) and hears "the clanking of his fetters – his silver fetters" (546). On his deathbed, Nostromo exclaims, "The silver has killed me. It has held me. It holds me yet" (559). Despite the continuing respect and admiration of those around him, Nostromo cannot be satisfied or at peace, knowing that he has sold himself for the silver. Emilia Gould most tellingly sums up the effect of the silver on all of Sulaco when she says to Monygham, "Isn't there enough treasure . . . to make everybody in the world miserable?" (557).

The result of the harsh judgment that Conrad passes on so many of his characters in *Nostromo* is much like what appears in *Lord Jim* and in so many of his other works. In *Lord Jim*, idealism came into question when Conrad demonstrated how Jim and others privilege it over human relationships. A similar effect occurs in *Nostromo*; in this case, though, it is the silver that is privileged over human relationships. This fact appears most clearly in the novel's characters, all of whose lives in some way or other revolve around the silver of the San Tomé mine.

The Secret Agent

The Secret Agent is perhaps Conrad's most perfectly constructed novel. His control of language and scene, as well as the ironic distance he achieves, combines with powerful moral and political issues to result in one of Conrad's finest works.

The novel opens with Adolf Verloc, the owner of a pornography shop and informant against London's revolutionary community, going to meet with Mr. Vladimir, a high-ranking diplomat of a foreign (probably Russian) embassy. Mr. Vladimir demands that Verloc blow up the Greenwich Meridian Observatory so that the revolutionaries will be blamed. He wants an outraged British public to pressure its politicians into cracking down on revolutionaries, many of whom are foreign exiles orchestrating revolutionary activities in their home countries. Verloc has married his former landlady's daughter, Winnie, and Winnie, her mother, and her intellectually challenged brother, Stevie, live with Verloc. After a few weeks, Verloc secures a bomb from the Professor, a notorious Anarchist. Worried over what he has been required to do, Verloc has begun going on long walks with Stevie. It is during this process that Verloc gets the idea that he will have Stevie place the bomb because he would attract no suspicion. When the time comes, however, Stevie apparently trips and blows himself to pieces. The police eventually find their way to Verloc because Winnie had sewn Stevie's address into a tag in his coat. Verloc confesses to the police and awaits his fate, having previously withdrawn all of his savings and given it to Winnie for safekeeping. Winnie, who adores her brother, overhears Verloc's confession, becomes distraught, and later stabs Verloc to death while he is lying on the couch. Afraid of being hanged, she leaves the house, intent on throwing herself into the Thames. On the way, she encounters Comrade Ossipon, one of Verloc's revolutionary acquaintances and a notorious womanizer. Winnie offers to run away with him, and after accompanying her back to her house, Ossipon discovers Verloc dead. Frightened, he develops a plan to get rid of Winnie. He suggests that they enter the train separately and then later meet up and take the ferry across the English Channel. Winnie gives Ossipon the money Verloc had given her, and after buying the train tickets he waits until Winnie gets onto the train. At the last moment, Ossipon leaps off the train, leaving Winnie to go on by herself. Later, Winnie drowns herself in the crossing. The novel ends with Ossipon tormented by the knowledge of what has happened.

The Secret Agent investigates the seedy underworld of London's radical politics in which revolutionaries and Anarchists work against mainstream Western civilization. Conrad is clearly contemptuous of these radicals. Comrade Ossipon, Michaelis, Karl Yundt, Adolf Verloc, and the Professor are members of the radical camp. Their politics range from being double agents to revolutionaries to terrorists to Anarchists. Each comes off poorly in Conrad's depiction. Verloc is lazy and conceited, and is also politically ineffective, which causes Mr. Vladimir to demand "a series of outrages" (28) from him. Furthermore, Verloc works as a double agent. But his most damning shortcoming is that he manages to get his brother-in-law blown up. Michaelis, on the other hand, spends his time writing a voluminous, incomprehensible memoir, while Karl Yundt is portrayed as a "swaggering spectre" (45) and "a disgusting old man" (50), who is "nursed by a blear-eyed old woman, a woman he had years ago enticed away from a friend, and afterwards had tried more than once to shake off into the gutter," but he cannot throw off this "indomitable snarling old witch" (45). As for Ossipon, Conrad ridicules his devotion to the ideas of Cesare Lombroso, and Ossipon seems more interested in seducing women than in engaging in politics. The final blow against him comes in his stealing Winnie's money and abandoning her to her death. The Professor is in some ways portrayed as the most politically committed of the group. He is referred to as "the perfect anarchist" (67), and in many ways he is. His sole goal is to blow up established society and start again. Conrad criticizes his views, but, more important, the Professor's views are tainted with his own personal disappointment; thus, his agenda appears to be largely his way of getting back at the world.

Given such a negative portrait of the political radicals in the novel, one might assume that Conrad sides with the established governments, but he does not. At least, he does not side with them except perhaps to suggest that they are a poor alternative to the revolutionaries and Anarchists. His attitude is particularly apparent in his portrait of Mr. Vladimir, who undoubtedly is meant to represent the unnamed Russian government. Mr. Vladimir's cynicism in ordering Verloc to blow up the Greenwich Meridian Observatory is particularly heinous since he is not making a political statement but simply seeking to throw blame for the incident onto the revolutionaries. Even though the bombing is unsuccessful, it still produces much of the effect for which Mr. Vladimir had hoped, since an outcry is raised against the revolutionaries. Furthermore, the bombing results in the deaths of Stevie, Verloc, and Winnie. The way Conrad intimately acquaints the reader with the Verloc family and their plight makes their fate (which is directly linked to Mr. Vladimir's demands) particularly poignant, but none of this matters to Mr. Vladimir, who is unconcerned with the human cost of his actions.

Conrad further demonstrates his disapproval of the established governments in his portrayal of Sir Ethelred and his secretary, Toodles, and in his portrayal of the British police. Despite his important political position, Sir Ethelred appears to be a fool (as does Toodles). Nor does the political infighting and the way that Chief Inspector Heat and the Assistant Commissioner attempt to circumvent each other present a coherent effort or one that is philosophically committed to the suppression of crime, as each man seeks to outdo the other and avoid being shown up. Worse, though, is the way they handle Verloc's murder, which appears to have been covered up at the end of the novel. The police seem to make no investigation into its cause or perpetrator. Furthermore, they use Verloc in the same way as Mr. Vladimir does. Verloc provides them with information in exchange for their looking the other way toward his questionable activities. In fact, in some ways, the government authorities and the political radicals seem more similar than different. Both groups eschew legal barriers to obtain what they want. In the end, Mr. Vladimir's and British police's use of Verloc differs little from Verloc's use of Stevie. Each casts aside considerations of individuals in pursuing political ends.

The Secret Agent is the second of Conrad's overtly political novels. Unlike *Nostromo*, which was set in developing Latin America, *The Secret Agent* is set in the very heart of Western civilization. The importance of the setting in *The Secret Agent* cannot be overemphasized. That the events of the novel occur where they do, allows Conrad to comment on both revolutionary activities as well as on Western civilization itself. As was true of the setting at the opening of "Heart of Darkness," at the time in which *The Secret Agent* is set, England was the most powerful nation on earth, both economically and politically. It was also the largest nation in the world, if one includes all of its colonial territories. Furthermore, as noted earlier, it viewed itself, and was viewed by others, as the height of Western civilization and civilized progress, and London was the epicenter of England's political, economic, and cultural progress. The fact that anarchy and chaos exist in this location is deeply ironic. Conrad often takes European characters and places them outside a Western setting in order to see how they will respond. Typically, once outside civilization, they become wholly uncivilized. In his works set outside Western civilization, Conrad reveals the inherent disorder of the world and thereby shows the order of Western civilization to be merely a facade imposed on a non-Western setting. In *The Secret Agent*, however, Conrad reveals anarchy and chaos in the very heart of Western civilization. By setting the novel in London, Conrad shows that even the seeming order of civilization in the West is illusory, as both political radicals and political conservatives work counter to social order.

As he does in his other political novels, Conrad also juxtaposes political issues against human issues. In *The Secret Agent*, radical politics intermingle with the Verloc family's attempts to exist in a world in which, as Winnie concludes, "things do not stand much looking into" (136). During the course of the novel, Conrad chronicles Winnie's life from the time she was a young girl until the time the novel is set and demonstrates that throughout her life she has had to make compromises. As a young girl, she protected Stevie from her father's violence, placing herself in harm's way by doing so. As a young woman, she fell in love with the butcher's son but was forced to give him up because of her responsibilities to her brother and infirm mother. In the end, she marries Verloc not because she loves him but because he represents financial security and because he is willing to let Winnie's mother and brother live with them. Hers is more of a business transaction than a romance, she providing the services of a wife for Verloc in exchange for him providing the services of husband for herself and her family. Winnie makes this choice because society presents her with no viable alternatives. Similarly, Winnie's mother applies for charity retirement housing thinking that Verloc will be less burdened with only Stevie and Winnie to support. Again, social circumstances dictate her self-sacrifice. In the plight of Winnie and her mother, we see Conrad's commentary on the desperate circumstances of women, particularly working-class and middle-class women.

Along with the plight of women, Conrad's juxtaposing the political and human plot lines serves to link the two such that they become inextricable and share not only the same participants but also the same plot lines. In other words, by employing two intertwining plot lines, Conrad forces the reader to compare and contrast them. The result is the human toll of the political activism. The senseless attempt on the Greenwich Observatory brings about the deaths of the three members of Verloc family. Despite the irony of Conrad's narrative voice, despite Verloc's incompetent machinations, despite Winnie's and Stevie's obscurity in British society, the reader sympathizes with the human tragedy that results from the politics. Conrad makes a good choice when he includes Stevie among his characters. In the end, Conrad shows that even an individual like Stevie, whom many would have seen to be a very small contributor to society, is worthy of value and sympathy. Verloc never recognizes this fact. Verloc was "under the mistaken impression that the value of individuals consists in what they are in themselves, he could not possibly comprehend the value of Stevie in the eyes of Mrs. Verloc" (177). It is Winnie's realization that Verloc could see no value in Stevie, as much as Verloc's actual role in Stevie's death, that causes her to murder him.

In the end, as is so often true in Conrad, the human becomes much more important than the idea or the object. The ideals of the political radicals and political conservatives fall by the wayside, while the value of human existence and the struggle for human survival takes precedence in *The Secret Agent*.

A Set of Six

Critical opinion on the stories in this volume has been mixed, with most commentators considering them to be lesser works, but this view is not wholly borne out, as a variety of interesting issues arise in this collection.

"The Brute" is a story about a ship, *The Apse Family*, that seems to bring about someone's death on every trip. On one trip in particular, the captain's wife and niece are aboard, and the niece, who has fallen in love with the chief mate, is killed when she is thrown overboard by a piece of the ship's machinery. Later, in a kind of poetic justice, the ship is run aground when Wilmot, the second mate, leaves his post while flirting with a female passenger. The story's primary significance lies in its narrative method and in its feminine terminology. "The Brute" contains one of the most striking examples of Conrad's attempt to place the reader in the place of the characters' experience. The story opens with the narrator entering the Three Crows bar and hearing another character remark:

> That fellow Wilmot fairly dashed her brains out, and a good job, too! . . .
> I was glad when I heard she got the knock from somebody at last.
> Sorry enough for poor Wilmot, though. That man and I used to be
> chums at one time. Of course that was the end of him. A clear case if
> there ever was one. No way out of it. None at all.   (105–6)

Not until several pages later, however, do the narrator and the reader discover
that the speaker was referring to a ship and not a woman. The effect of this
narrative technique is, of course, that both the narrator and the reader
mistake the subject of conversation, and the reader experiences the events
as if he or she were in the place of the narrator at the exact moment the
conversation occurs. This conversation also points to a pattern that occurs
throughout the story of associating *The Apse Family* with women, and
hence the changeable and murderous nature of the ship is projected onto
the female characters and onto women in general, thus implying that women
pose a threat to the male world of the sea – and perhaps the male world in
general. Such a view of women opens up various possibilities for analyzing
the role of women in the world of the sea, and as was true in *The Rescue*,
"The Brute" seems to represent women as a disruptive element in male
communities.

"Il Conde" is a tale of lost innocence. Living in Naples for his health, a
Count (probably Polish) lives a life of cultured comfort, pleasure, and safety
until one evening when he is robbed at knife point. He only loses a small
amount of money and an inexpensive watch, but after the thief leaves, the
Count realizes that he had forgotten about a gold coin that he carries in case
of an emergency. Shortly thereafter, he goes to a café to get something to eat
and to calm his nerves and he is again accosted by the thief, who accuses the
Count of deceitfully withholding the gold coin. The thief verbally abuses
the Count before leaving. Devastated, the Count confesses to the narrator
that he can no longer live in Naples. The two encounters succeed in destroy-
ing the Count's world, but for different reasons. The first encounter rudely
awakens him from his life of comfort and safety such that he can never feel
safe again. In this incident, Conrad demonstrates again the fact that human
beings ultimately cannot control their environment. The later encounter,
although further solidifying the effect of the earlier one, affects the Count's
view of the world in a different way. In this case, the thief questions the
Count's honor and integrity, in effect accusing him of being dishonest. With
his honor in question and with his cultured and comfortable existence
shattered, the Count can no longer face living in Naples and leaves to go to
what will likely be his death.

"The Duel" is set in Napoleonic France and is the tale of a duel between D'Hubert and Feraud, two officers in the French army. D'Hubert is sent to place Feraud under house arrest because of Feraud's involvement in a duel with a civilian. Feraud considers this an insult and challenges D'Hubert to a duel. Over the course of a number of years, the two fight a series of duels (always instigated by Feraud) in which each combatant is wounded but not killed. After Napoleon's defeat, Feraud challenges D'Hubert to a final duel. When Feraud misses with both shots, D'Hubert claims Feraud's life as forfeit but spares him, thus ending the duel.

Many commentators have considered this tale to be a slight one, but several issues are of interest. As he does with the narrator in "Falk" and Razumov, Conrad presents a character, D'Hubert, who finds himself in an untenable situation in which he is the victim of an irrational and absurd world. He feels helpless to escape from the nightmarish duel: "For years General D'Hubert had been exasperated and humiliated by an atrocious absurdity imposed upon him by this man's [Feraud's] savage caprice" (256). As happens elsewhere, Conrad emphasizes the fact that human beings have limited control of their existence. Furthermore, a subtle questioning of Western values appears in the story. The duel proceeds within an accepted code of behavior in a civilized community, but Conrad seems to question such a view. He presents the duel as a nightmare as D'Hubert remarks, "It was all like a very wicked and harassing dream" (182). D'Hubert finally concludes, "The problem was how to kill the adversary. Nothing short of that would free him from this imbecile nightmare" (251). The irrationality of the duel (which the dream imagery underscores) as well as the fact that these men are trying to kill one another over a code of honor both bring Western values into question, and their behavior seems anything but civilized. In this story, as elsewhere, Conrad is suspicious of any idea that takes precedence of human beings and human life, particularly an idea with as little justification as the duel, which has no basis except in Feraud's mind. If only Feraud accepted the justification for the duel, then Conrad would merely be commenting on Feraud's irrationality. Everyone else in the story, however, also accepts the necessity of the duel. Feraud never explains why he challenges D'Hubert, and D'Hubert refuses to say, reluctantly fighting Feraud whenever challenged. With an approving community standing witness, both men risk their lives for no reason. Conrad it seems portrays not a civilized world but rather one gone mad. He further critiques the duel when the last challenge occurs just before D'Hubert is to marry. While D'Hubert is a victim of Feraud's irrationality, he does not have to engage Feraud this final time. A quiet word to the authorities, and Feraud would have been back under house arrest, never knowing D'Hubert's role in his capture. Instead, D'Hubert in effect makes the same choice that Jim does: choosing an issue of honor over a human bond. D'Hubert is simply luckier than Jim and does not die in the process. Nevertheless, given his impending wedding as well as his knowledge of the duel's baselessness, D'Hubert's decision to meet Feraud's challenge appears even more suspect than does Jim's decision at the end of *Lord Jim*.

"Gaspar Ruiz" is perhaps the least substantive story in this collection. Written shortly after *Nostromo*, it is set in South America but contains none of *Nostromo*'s scope or complexity. Gaspar Ruiz is a simple, strong man, unjustly condemned to the firing squad for deserting the revolutionary forces. Somehow he survives and is nursed back to health by a young aristocratic Royalist woman. The revolutionaries have ruined her family, and the woman wants to avenge their loss. Ruiz avoids recapture as a result of an earthquake, during which he saves the lives of the woman and General Robles, who had sought to capture Ruiz. As a result, Ruiz is pardoned and soon rises to a prominent position among the revolutionaries. The woman, who has now become Ruiz's wife, however, spurs him to avenge her losses, and Ruiz rises up against the revolutionary forces and begins a war of revenge against them. Later, the revolutionaries capture Ruiz's wife and daughter. During the rescue attempt, the cannon mounting breaks, and Ruiz serves as a human mount, having the cannon placed on his back. The rescue is successful, but Ruiz's back is broken in the process, and he dies just after hearing his wife profess her love for him. Shortly thereafter, she commits suicide by leaping into a chasm. "Gaspar Ruiz" considers the issue of betrayal that appears so often in Conrad's works, and, as is true elsewhere, betrayal in "Gaspar Ruiz" represents a breach of community. Somewhat unique to this story, though, the issue of betrayal is linked to politics, more specifically political betrayal, as Gaspar is betrayed by both the revolutionaries and the Royalists. In this fact, we see Conrad once again demonstrating his suspicion of politics in general as he rejects both revolutionary and conservative politics. Conrad shows how the individual is so often caught between such larger forces, as Ruiz is the victim of both Royalists and revolutionaries and is sacrificed to their political ends.

"The Informer" is an account of Anarchism and is an interesting precursor to *The Secret Agent* and *Under Western Eyes*. The story concerns an Anarchist group that is patronized by an aristocratic woman who seems to see it all as a game. One of the Anarchists, Sevrin, falls in love with her. The group later discovers that an informer has infiltrated them, and so they set a trap in which they stage a fake raid on the house where they work. In the process,

Sevrin, who turns out to be the informer, gives himself up out of fear that the Professor upstairs will detonate a bomb, killing the woman he loves. In this story, Conrad presents an example of an individual who rejects an idea (loyalty to the police) in favor of preserving the woman he loves (unworthy as she is of his devotion). As almost always occurs in Conrad's works, human relationships are more important than ideas. "The Informer" is also significant in its depiction of Anarchism. The narrator of the story has a perfect horror of Anarchists and considers them to be madmen. He says, "anarchists in general were simply inconceivable to me mentally, morally, logically, sentimentally, and even physically" (97). One evening, though, he meets Mr. X, an Anarchist who relates Sevrin's tale, and the narrator finds the experience extremely troubling. He contemplates Mr. X and thinks, "He was alive and European; he had the manner of good society, wore a coat and hat like mine, and had pretty near the same taste in cooking. It was too frightful to think of" (76). What frightens the narrator is that Mr. X reminds him of himself and represents the undermining of the narrator's Western values and society not by some madman but rather by someone very much like himself.

"The Anarchist" is a somewhat misnamed tale about a man who is labeled an Anarchist but who is clearly nothing of the sort. Paul, a Parisian workman, is celebrating his birthday one night at a restaurant and has too much to drink. Anarchists at a neighboring table fire his anger with tales of social injustice, which eventually lead to Paul shouting Anarchist slogans. Paul and the Anarchists are arrested, and he is convicted and sent to jail. Upon his release, he can no longer find work in France because of his reputation. Eventually, he falls in with Anarchists and participates in a bank robbery. Arrested again, he is sentenced to prison on St. Joseph's island. At one point, a riot breaks out, and Paul finds a gun and a small boat. Two Anarchists join him in his escape, but when a rescue boat comes in sight Paul shoots the Anarchists and throws their bodies overboard. At the time of the story, Paul is employed by Harry Gee, who exploits him, spreading rumors about his Anarchism so that he cannot leave the island on which they live and find work elsewhere.

The tale presents a character, like Razumov, D'Hubert, and the narrator of "Falk," who finds himself in a situation beyond his control. As a punishment for his drunken statements against social injustice, he is sent to jail and then can no longer find work. In this way, the story emphasizes the irrationality and absurdity of human existence. "The Anarchist" also comments on the idea of politics, particularly radical politics. During the course of the story, the main character is used by the Anarchists and his lawyer for political ends without regard for the consequences. Conrad criticizes the Anarchists in the story, much as he does elsewhere in his fiction. As he does in those instances, however, Conrad's critique of radical politics does not imply his endorsing conservative politics. At the beginning of the story, the French authorities put Paul in jail on the basis of drunken statements, and at the end of the story Harry Gee, an arch anti-Anarchist, exploits Paul just as much as the Anarchists did earlier in the story.

Under Western Eyes

Under Western Eyes is perhaps Conrad's most human novel, in that it most clearly opposes human relations and emotions against fixed ideas. The third and last of Conrad's overtly political novels, it is usually considered to be among his best works.

The novel is a kind of frame narrative in which an unnamed British teacher of foreign languages reconstructs events in the life of Kirylo Sidor-ovitch Razumov. The tale begins with Razumov, a student at St. Petersburg University, preparing to write an essay that he hopes will win a medal and thus guarantee the success of his future career. Razumov is a young man without ties. He has no family, although he is the unacknowledged illegitim-ate son of Prince K——. Razumov is also without any significant ties to politics, but his independence from politics abruptly changes. On returning to his rooms one evening, he discovers a fellow student, Victor Haldin, waiting for him. Haldin has assassinated a political official and evaded capture. He comes to Razumov believing him to be sympathetic to the cause. In reality, Razu-mov is only mildly sympathetic and is considerably disturbed by Haldin's presence. Razumov recognizes that he would be seen as a co-conspirator, his career ruined, should Haldin be discovered. Wishing to rid himself of Haldin, Razumov agrees to help him escape by arranging for a sleigh driver, Ziemianitch, to spirit him away. The plan falls through when Razumov discovers the driver in a drunken slumber. Feeling hopelessly compromised, Razumov convinces himself that he abhors Haldin and his actions and determines to turn in Haldin to the authorities. After betraying Haldin, guilt haunts Razumov. Unable to return to his previous existence, in the end, Razumov decides to work for the authorities as a double agent infiltrating the ex-patriot revolutionary center in Geneva. Razumov convinces himself that he is protecting Russia from revolutionary activities, but he is also motivated by revenge against Haldin and his associates. Razumov is remarkably suc-cessful in winning the confidence of the revolutionaries and begins reporting on their activities. In Geneva, Razumov also meets Nathalia Haldin, Victor's sister, and is eventually won over by her pure and honest personality. Troubled by lingering guilt over his betrayal of Haldin, and motivated by Nathalia's frank honesty, Razumov determines to confess his role in Haldin's capture, first to Nathalia and then to the ex-patriot revolutionaries. As a result of his confession, Nikita, a brutal member of the revolutionaries (and a double agent), bursts Razumov's eardrums. After this, unable to hear an oncoming streetcar, Razumov is run over and severely injured. Once recovered enough from his injuries to leave the hospital, Razumov returns to Russia, living out what remains of his life in the rural countryside.

Under Western Eyes focuses on four major issues: moral and psychological conflict, politics, human relationships, and the Western perception of the East. Although *Under Western Eyes* is a political novel, it is primarily, as are so many of Conrad's other works, a novel about moral and psychological conflict. Razumov experiences this conflict as he wrestles with the consequences of his betrayal of Haldin. When Razumov initially betrays him to the authorities, he thinks he has done the right thing, feeling that Haldin had killed people and had directly threatened Razumov himself by threatening Russia. Razumov then believes he can go back to his life before the incident, but he cannot. Although he is unable to admit it to himself, Razumov is racked with guilt almost from the outset and finds he can no longer concentrate on his studies, ultimately giving them up and turning instead to revenge against those whom he believes have ruined his life. In the end, though, his struggle against guilt is too much for him, and he concludes, "perdition is my lot" (362).

Conrad, however, wishes us to see beyond Razumov's personal plight. As he does so often, Conrad employs individual characters to comment on humanity as a whole, and in *Under Western Eyes* we see the workings of Conrad's view of the universe and the nature of human existence as well. Razumov is consistently subject to the whims of fate and shows little or no control over his existence. He is helpless to prevent Haldin's drawing him into the revolutionary conflict, and the atmosphere of suspicion that surrounds all of Russian society further prevents Razumov from avoiding involvement. He believes that he will be found complicit in the bombing and his career will be wrecked in the process. Seeking to control his existence, he decides to betray Haldin, but in so doing he does nothing to avoid the fate he had feared and in fact ends up worse. His career is ruined, and he becomes a haunted creature. At other junctures in the novel, Razumov again is at the mercy of fate. Had Ziemianitch not been drunk, perhaps Razumov might have been able to escape his predicament, but chance would have it that Ziemianitch chose that particular night to get drunk. Later, we learn that after his interview with Razumov regarding Haldin, Councillor Mikulin "would have simply dropped him [Razumov] for ever" (306) – except for another quirk of fate. Mikulin assumes another position in the government and realizes that he can make good use of Razumov: "He saw great possibilities of special usefulness in that uncommon young man on whom he had a hold already" (307). Later, that Razumov and Natalia Haldin happen to be in the same city, that Nikita happens to be present when Razumov confesses, and, perhaps most symbolically, that Razumov happens to wander out in front of the streetcar just when it happens to be traveling past, all combine to demonstrate the lack of control Razumov has over his existence and the fact that even when he tries to control his life, as when he chooses to confess or chooses to betray Haldin, he seems unable to change anything about his fate. He is buffeted about by the winds of chance and can do nothing to avoid it. In Razumov's example, Conrad seems to be making a more general statement about the nature of the universe and of human existence itself. Like Razumov, human beings find themselves in a world in which they believe they can control their lives, but in reality political and social entities eliminate much of their ability to do so, and, even more disturbing, human beings have no control over what events will occur that may draw them in and forever alter their existence. This theme appears frequently throughout Conrad's writings.

The political issues that Conrad tackles in *Under Western Eyes* are also familiar ones: autocracy and revolution. Conrad investigates the workings of the Russian government and the machinations of its revolutionary opponents. During the course of the novel, Conrad reveals a government that protects its power jealously and seems to work outside established laws. The result is a bureaucracy that fosters suspicion, intrigue, and repression. To Western eyes, Haldin's arrival in Razumov's rooms should presage nothing more than some inconvenience, since Razumov was not involved in the assassination. The novel is set in Russia, however, and Razumov immediately sees his situation as nearly hopeless. He knows that if anyone were to see Haldin coming or leaving he would be implicated and his future ruined. As it is, even though Razumov does the government a great service by turning Haldin in, he remains under suspicion, and in the end his future is destroyed just as he had feared. Similarly, despite Mikulin's good service to the government, he also is later destroyed:

> during one of those State trials which astonish and puzzle the average plain man who reads the newspapers, by a glimpse of unsuspected intrigues. And in the stir of vaguely seen monstrosities, in that momentary, mysterious disturbance of muddy waters, Councillor

> Mikulin went under, dignified, with only a calm, emphatic protest of his
> innocence – nothing more.   (305)

Accusations, whether false or true, can ruin a person, and Razumov must try
to negotiate precisely such a precarious environment when he discovers
Haldin in his rooms.

Given his indictment of Russian autocracy, one might expect Conrad's
sympathies to lie with the revolutionaries – but they do not. Unlike many
political novels (but typical of Conrad's politics), he condemns both sides.
Conrad portrays the revolutionaries as ineffectual, deranged, or wrong-
headed. Peter Ivanovitch may be good with theoretical politics (although
Conrad represents his views as silly), but he seems ineffective with practical
politics. In fact, this disparity is most apparent when he engages in his
theoretical work. While dictating his ideas on the betterment of humanity,
Peter Ivanovitch treats Tekla as little better than a slave. Similarly, Madame de
S— appears ghoulish and not wholly sane, and although she may support the
revolutionaries while alive, she fails to provide for them when dead. Finally,
Nikita is a double agent and a "fiend" (as Sophia Antonovna calls him) who
enjoys killing and brutality. Nor do the revolutionary students come off
much better. Kostia is an ineffectual fool, and the red-nosed student and
Haldin are described as being intoxicated with idealistic dreams (31). Perhaps
the most telling evidence of Conrad's position regarding the revolutionaries,
however, has to do with the assassination itself, in which Conrad carefully
chronicles the fact that a number of innocent bystanders die in the attack.
This incident serves as a microcosm of Conrad's primary point: in the
crossfire between the autocratic government and the revolutionary cause
the innocent become the greatest victims.

In the novel, both the revolutionaries and the Russian government
come off poorly, as each digests and then discards enemies, friends, and
bystanders alike. Each camp tramples humanity in the progress of its cause.
Conrad expresses his most pessimistic views in his "Author's Note" to the
novel:

> The ferocity and imbecility of an autocratic rule rejecting all legality and
> in fact basing itself upon complete moral anarchism provokes the no
> less imbecile and atrocious answer of a purely Utopian revolutionism
> encompassing destruction by the first means to hand, in the strange
> conviction that a fundamental change of hearts must follow the
> downfall of any given human institutions. These people are unable to
> see that all they can effect is merely a change of names. The oppressors
> and the oppressed are all Russians together; and the world is brought

once more face to face with the truth of the saying that the tiger cannot change his stripes nor the leopard his spots.   (x)

Conrad further shows his contempt for autocracy and revolution when the narrator remarks, "It seems that the savage autocracy, no more than the divine democracy, does not limit its diet exclusively to the bodies of its enemies. It devours its friends and servants as well" (306). In this volatile political climate, Razumov tries to avoid taking sides. He simply wants to be left alone to pursue his studies and accomplish his apolitical goals. The political world of revolution and autocracy, however, does not allow for neutrality, and Razumov is alternately swept up first onto one side and then onto the other, ultimately discovering that he can escape neither and is in the end crushed between them.

Conrad also investigates this political world of revolution and autocracy by presenting these events from the narrator's perspective, a Western European, who views the actions of Eastern Europeans through the eyes of the West. Conrad represents a fundamental difference between the world of the East and the world of the West, one which most Westerners cannot comprehend and can only see from their own perspective. In this way, Conrad attempts to demonstrate that Eastern Europe is distinct from Western Europe, but at the same time, Conrad indicts the West for its insistence on viewing the world solely through its own eyes and for its inability to see any other perspective.

Set against this world of politics, though, is the world of human relations. This world first appears in the character of Ziemianitch. Razumov is told, "Saint or devil, night or day is all one to Ziemianitch when his heart is free from sorrow" (29), but in so saying the keeper of the eating-house identifies Ziemianitch's priorities. Dedicated as he may be to the revolutionary cause, human relations take precedence. The narrator remarks that "Ziemianitch's passionate surrender to sorrow and consolation had baffled" Razumov (31), and Razumov himself notes that Ziemianitch's drunkenness results from lost love rather than from the "dream-intoxication of the idealist" (31). Ziemianitch seals his views with his suicide later in the novel – resulting not from political disappointment but rather from despair over losing a woman (275–6).

The novel also takes up the story of Haldin's mother and his sister living in Geneva and awaiting word of Victor. Their emotional attachment and dependency on Victor is clear, and this relationship stands in sharp contrast to the political world that swirls about them. For them, politics matter little. The touching picture of their devotion to Victor, as well as Natalia's devotion to her mother, diverge from the cold and often brutal political world. Politics drastically disrupts their lives, however, when they learn that Victor has been executed for assassinating Mr. de P——. Victor's mother despairs, and so when Natalia learns that Razumov (of whom Victor has remarked favorably) has come to Geneva, she is anxious to meet him, hoping to learn something of her brother's fate and ideally finding something with which to comfort her mother.

Tekla also represents human emotion juxtaposed against political ideas. Razumov first meets her while visiting the Château Borel. Tekla's situation there is terrible, and she tells Razumov, "I have been starving for, I won't say kindness, but just for a little civility, for I don't know how long" (233). She has been mistreated by Peter Ivanovitch and the other revolutionaries and says, "Yes, if you were to get ill, or meet some bitter trouble, you would find I am not a useless fool. You have only to let me know. I will come to you. I will indeed. And I will stick to you" (233). Tekla is a committed revolutionary, but for her, revolution is not theoretical and removed from humanity (as it appears to be with Peter Ivanovitch and the others) but rather intimately connected with human beings. She demonstrates her views in her service to "poor Andrei," for whom she left a comfortable existence with her middle-class family to live in squalor rather than accept the human misery that resulted from the bureaucracy of which her family was a part. For her, the revolution is to serve human beings, and she pledges to do just that, later following through with her commitment when she assumes care of Razumov after his accident.

The most important example, though, of Conrad's emphasis on the pre-eminence of humanity over ideas appears in the relationship between Natalia and Razumov. As noted earlier, when Natalia hears that Razumov has come to Geneva, she wants to meet him in hopes that he can provide some comfort for her and her mother. Razumov's feelings are quite different, however. In a journal entry written to Natalia, he comments on Victor and Natalia, "I believed that I had in my breast nothing but an inexhaustible fund of anger and hate for you both . . . And do you know what I said to myself? I shall steal his sister's soul from her" (358–9). In the end, though, Razumov recognizes the simple purity of Natalia's being and the genuine emotional attachment she has for her brother and for Razumov as well. This results in a change of heart: "It was as if your pure brow bore a light which fell on me, searched my heart and saved me from ignominy, from ultimate undoing. And it saved you too . . . I felt that I must tell you that I had ended by loving you" (361). Razumov had tried to convince himself that he opposed the revolutionaries on conviction and thought his desire for revenge took precedence over all else, but he discovers instead that ideas, such as patriotism and revenge, matter little when compared to genuine human attachment. Later, Sophia Antonovna remarks:

> It was just when he believed himself safe and more – infinitely more – when the possibility of being loved by that admirable girl first dawned upon him, that he discovered that his bitterest railings, the worst wickedness, the devil work of his hate and pride, could never cover up the ignominy of the existence before him. There's character in such a discovery. (380)

Razumov himself expresses this same conclusion when he writes, "In giving Victor Haldin up, it was myself, after all, whom I have betrayed most basely" (361). In the end, humanity matters more than ideas, something Razumov had not originally realized. Even Peter Ivanovitch seems to come to a similar conclusion. When Sophia Antonovna tells the narrator "Peter Ivanovitch has united himself to a peasant girl," the narrator exclaims, "Is he, then, living actually in Russia? It's a tremendous risk – isn't it? And all for the sake of a peasant girl. Don't you think it's very wrong of him?" But she merely answers, "He just simply adores her" (381–2). In the end, Peter Ivanovitch gives up his role as leader of the ex-patriot revolutionaries to live his life out in obscurity with the woman he loves. He, too, chooses human bonds over political ideas.

If there is a bright spot in this otherwise bleak tale, it is that Razumov achieves a moral victory. At the crucial moment, Razumov chose humanity over ideas, and so although Razumov lives what is left of his life in obscurity, crippled and deaf, he has become a much more complete person than he was earlier when he turned his back on humanity and betrayed Haldin and then became consumed with misguided ideas of patriotism, hate, and revenge.

'Twixt Land and Sea

In this collection of stories, Conrad returns once again to the sea after a lengthy hiatus. Critics and readers at the time applauded this return, and the collection became Conrad's most financially successful book up until that time.

Although all three stories are set in the world of the sea, "The Secret Sharer" is less about events external to the individual than those that are internal. Considered to be among Conrad's finest short stories, the tale begins with a young captain unsure of himself in his first command. One evening, while alone on deck, he notices a man hanging onto the ship's ladder. The man, Leggatt, turns out to be the first mate of the *Sephora*. Leggatt had killed an insubordinate crew member during a storm and was being transported to Bankok to stand trial when he escaped. The young captain feels a strange affinity for Leggatt and hides him in his own quarters. The next day, Captain Archibold of the *Sephora* arrives looking for Leggatt, but the young captain does not reveal Leggatt's presence. Several days later, the captain comes up with a plan to help Leggatt. Since the ship has been becalmed, he brings it dangerously close to shore on the pretext of trying to catch land breezes. His real intent, however, is to give Leggatt his best chance of being able to swim to land. During a tense scene in which the ship's officers believe the captain to have gone insane, Leggatt slips down the ship's ladder and swims away. Luckily, the captain spots the hat he had given Leggatt floating on the water where it had fallen off. The young captain is then able to use the hat as a marker and successfully right the ship in time. An unexpected result of this maneuver is that the captain gains the respect of the crew, who now assume that he knew exactly what he was doing all along.

"The Secret Sharer" is the psychological study of an unnamed young captain's struggle to demonstrate to himself that he is worthy to command. More than this, though, the story is an investigation into the process by which one attempts to come to a knowledge of oneself. Early in the story, the young captain remarks, "But what I felt most was my being a stranger to the ship; and if all the truth must be told, I was somewhat of a stranger to myself" (93). Like the young captain, all human beings imagine how they will respond to challenges. Jim does this in *Lord Jim*, but unlike Jim, the captain remarks, "I wondered how far I should turn out faithful to that ideal conception of one's own personality every man sets up for himself secretly" (94). Untested by circumstances, the young captain wonders how he will respond when challenged. The story, then, is the captain's journey toward fulfilling the role with which he has been entrusted. To do so, he must demonstrate to himself and to his crew that he can command and meet challenges. Leggatt is one of these challenges. As the narrator remarks, "In this breathless pause at the threshold of a long passage we seemed to be measuring our [his and his ship's] fitness for a long and arduous enterprise, the appointed task of both our existences to be carried out, far from all human eyes, with only sky and sea for spectators and for judges" (92). With the crew unaware of Leggatt's existence, no outside forces can see or judge the captain's actions. He must face the challenges and make the decisions alone. On the surface, the case seems quite straightforward. Leggatt has committed a crime for which he was being held pending transfer to the proper judicial authorities. The captain's duty would seem to lie in Leggatt's return to the

Sephora. Because he feels an affinity for Leggatt, though, the young captain begins to sympathize with Leggatt's plight. Conrad is careful to note a number of ways in which Leggatt resembles the young captain, and in this way Leggatt becomes the captain's double or darker self. As a result, the young captain decides to help Leggatt, going so far as to conceal his presence from his crew and from the captain of the *Sephora*.

When the young captain first encounters Leggatt, he also encounters a moral dilemma. He must determine the degree of Leggatt's guilt, and he must determine his own responsibility to both Leggatt and the law. In the end, the captain comes to see mitigating circumstances in Leggatt's situation and chooses to act outside the requirements of the law, which are unyielding in requiring Leggatt to stand trial. Unlike Archibold, who believes that the only option is to give up Leggatt "to the law" (118), the young captain chooses to follow his own judgment and allows Leggatt to swim off quietly to the island of Koh-ring.

There has been much debate concerning the young captain's choice. Some have argued that Conrad sympathizes with the captain's choice to reject the unbending rule of law in favor of his own personal judgment – in a sense rejecting an idea over a humanity. Others argue that Conrad is critical of the captain's action because he disregards the law and places his ship in danger. Conrad leaves evidence to support both views, and there is no easy answer to this problem. In any case, though, before Leggatt accomplishes his escape, the captain must face a more practical challenge to his abilities. In giving Leggatt his best chance to swim to shore safely, the young captain tests to the limit his own abilities and those of his crew. Nevertheless, the result is that both he and his crew recognize him as captain and able to fulfill that role. Consequently, because of his experience with Leggatt, whereas the young captain was unsure of himself at the opening of the story, by the end of the story he has come to a greater knowledge of himself and his abilities.

"Freya of the Seven Isles" is a story of anti-melodrama. Freya Nelson, the daughter of a Danish tobacco planter, is in love with Jasper Allen, an English trader and the proud owner of a fine ship, the *Bonito*. A Dutch Lieutenant Heemskirk, however, wishes to have Freya for himself. At this time, the Dutch and English are competing fiercely for trade and territories in the region. Freya's father fears the Dutch authorities, and as a result Freya believes that her father will oppose her marriage to Allen, so she plans to elope with him on the day after her twenty-first birthday. Allen visits Freya one last time before their planned elopement, but while there Heemskirk happens to see them kiss. After Allen leaves, Heemskirk, insane with jealousy, makes advances toward Freya, at which point she slaps him. Freya's father comes upon them just after this, and Heemskirk is forced to leave in silent pain and fury. The next morning Heemskirk follows Allen's brig as it leaves the area and later detains it. Heemskirk thus discovers by chance that, unbeknownst to Allen, Schultz, Allen's mate, has sold firearms to some of the local inhabitants, Heemskirk then tows the *Bonito* to Makassar. On the way, however, he deliberately releases the tow rope so that the ship will run aground on a reef at high tide, making it impossible ever to salvage it. Heartbroken, Allen goes mad and spends his days staring at the wreck. Discovering Allen's condition, Freya eventually wastes away and dies.

This story has the elements of a melodrama complete with an evil villain (Heemskirk), good hero (Jasper Allen), and a romantic triangle, but even in his more pedestrian pieces Conrad is not content to follow the crowd. Although this story is a kind of melodrama, its conclusion is anything but melodramatic. Heemskirk prevails and suffers no consequences for his evil actions. In this overturning of the melodrama, Conrad makes a statement regarding the nature of good and evil in the world. Clearly, Conrad argues that no transcendental power directs the affairs of humanity and intercedes on their behalf. Instead, they are alone in the world and must confront their fate without hope of divine protection, without confidence that they live in a world of order and justice, and without the ability to exert any significant control over their lives. In asserting such ideas, "Freya of the Seven Isles" is certainly one of Conrad's bleakest tales.

"A Smile of Fortune" is an interesting contrast to "Freya of the Seven Isles." Both stories treat the question of fate in human existence, but each comes to a different conclusion. In "A Smile of Fortune," a young captain arrives at a tropical port intent on picking up a cargo of sugar. He carries a recommendation letter to a Mr. Jacobus, and as soon as the captain arrives a Mr. Jacobus greets him. It turns out, though, that this Mr. Jacobus is the brother (Alfred) of the man for whom the letter was meant (Ernest). The brothers are business rivals, and Alfred is an outcast in the community. Ernest is an unpleasant man, and the young captain begins spending time with Alfred while he waits for bags in which to load the sugar. While visiting Alfred, the captain meets Alfred's illegitimate daughter, Alice. The young captain becomes taken with the solitary young woman and one evening suddenly begins kissing her. Alice frees herself from the captain's embrace and flees the room. After she leaves, the young captain sees Alfred and assumes that he has witnessed the incident. The young captain and Alfred then work out an arrangement in which the captain will get the bags he needs if he will also accept a cargo of potatoes. The final surprise occurs when the captain arrives in Australia to discover that a shortage has caused the price of potatoes to skyrocket.

Unlike "Freya of the Seven Isles," in "A Smile of Fortune," Conrad shows the other side of fate when a young captain is forced to accept a cargo of potatoes and later unexpectedly makes a huge profit from them. Regardless of the difference in the outcome of the two stories, however, the message is the same: human beings can neither predict nor control the course of their lives. "A Smile of Fortune" also bears some similarity to "The Secret Sharer" in that in both stories a young captain must encounter difficulties and see whether he is equal to the test. In this story, the young captain seems less successful than the young captain in "The Secret Sharer." In addition to commenting on fate in human lives, "A Smile of Fortune" also considers the inequity of treatment in the cases of Alice and a mulatto boy. Ernest Jacobus abuses the mulatto boy, who is presumably his illegitimate son, but receives no social censure, unlike his brother Alfred, who is ostracized from society along with his illegitimate daughter Alice. Conrad exposes the hypocrisy of society as well as its racial bias. It seems that it is one thing to father out of wedlock a child with a non-Western woman but another thing entirely to father one with a Western woman.

The publication of *'Twixt Land and Sea* would mark the end of Conrad's most productive period and the period that most commentators feel represents Conrad's most important work. What would follow would engender numerous debates over why Conrad's later work diverged so much from his earlier work.

Chapter 5

Conrad's later period

Probably all readers have noted a distinct shift in Conrad's work that appeared after *Under Western Eyes*. Early assessments, such as that of Thomas C. Moser, Douglas Hewitt, and Albert J. Guerard, regarded this shift to be a decline in literary quality. Most readers would cite *The Shadow-Line* as a notable exception to any view of the differences between Conrad's later works and his earlier works. *Victory* is also cited as an exception at times, although opinion is much more widely divided over it. In addition, *Chance* has its supporters. For many years, most commentators on Conrad's works have tended to agree with the assessments of Moser, Guerard and others. Some notable exceptions were John A. Palmer, Daniel R. Schwarz, and Gary Geddes, who, in different ways, argued for a re-assessment of Conrad's later works, as have, more recently, Robert Hampson and Susan Jones, for example. Regardless of whether one sees Conrad's later works (excepting *The Shadow-Line* and perhaps *Victory*) as representing a decline in quality or whether one sees them as representing a shift in direction, it is impossible not to recognize that a difference exists between these works and those of his earlier periods.

Chance

Chance was Conrad's first financially successful novel and was generally well received by the critics and public when it was first published. The novel is the last of the Marlow narratives, and many commentators have felt that the Marlow who appears in this novel bears little resemblance to the Marlow of "Youth," "Heart of Darkness," and *Lord Jim*. *Chance* is largely the story of Flora de Barral, but it begins with her father, a man who rises in the financial world more from luck and the confidence he can inspire in others than through financial acumen. The result is as one might expect: de Barral's financial house of cards eventually comes crashing down, and he is sent to prison for fraud. Just before Flora's unscrupulous governess absconds with what little she can, she berates young Flora, telling her how useless and unloveable she is. Flora is devastated by this experience and becomes deeply depressed. Left alone, she is befriended by her neighbors the Fynes. Several years later, Marlow is staying in the country near the Fynes, and Marlow and Mr. Fyne become friends. Flora periodically stays with the Fynes and one day leaves, sending a letter to Mrs. Fyne telling her that she has run off with and intends to marry Mrs. Fyne's brother, Captain Anthony, whom she has met at the Fynes. Flora does not love Anthony but accepts his proposal nevertheless. The two marry just before Flora's father is released from prison, and Flora and her father then join Anthony on his ship. Flora's father has been greatly affected by his prison experience and resents the fact that Flora has married. He hates Anthony and life on the ship. One night, Powell, one of the ship's officers, happens to see into Anthony's cabin from a skylight and notices de Barral putting something into Anthony's drink while he has stepped away. Powell then goes down to warn Anthony. Confronted by the degree to which Flora's father hates him, and tormented by the thought that Flora does not love him, Anthony tells Flora that he will give her up, but Flora replies that she does not want to be given up. While Anthony escorts her back to bed, de Barral drinks the poisoned liquid, realizing that he cannot have Flora to himself. Some years later, Anthony dies in an accident, and the novel ends with the union of Flora and Powell.

Chance employs the most complicated narrative method among Conrad's later novels, and many commentators, beginning with Henry James, have wondered whether the novel simply privileges form over content. *Chance* certainly does not have the same bewildering narrative complexities of *Lord Jim* and *Nostromo*, for instance, but the narrative does move in both a linear and circular pattern, similar to Ford Madox Ford's contemporaneous *The Good Soldier*, and introduces continually more information each time the narrative circles back again. Unlike some of Conrad's earlier works, however, *Chance*'s narrative complexity does not seem to bear the weight of the moral and epistemological complexities of *Nostromo* and *Lord Jim*, in which form and content seem to reinforce one another.

All of this said, *Chance* certainly has points to recommend it. It is the most extended discussion of women and women's issues in Conrad's works, and, unlike any of Conrad's other novels, *Chance* is really a novel about a woman. The difficulty is in determining where Conrad comes down on the issue. On the one hand, Mrs. Fyne's feminist ideas come across quite negatively, and she is made to appear shrewish toward her husband and rabid in her views. Her views are further undermined by the fact that she seems to abandon them when they are inconvenient, particularly when Flora runs off with

Mrs. Fyne's brother. Flora is in effect simply following some of Mrs. Fyne's own views. On the other hand, Conrad deals with Flora and her plight with a great deal of sympathy, both because she has been treated poorly by life but also because she has been treated poorly because of her position as a woman. In the latter case, Conrad seems to be sympathizing with the plight of women in society.

Chance also takes up an issue that appears throughout Conrad's work: the idea of chance itself. The title comes from the idea that so much that occurs in the novel results from chance. Some of the chance happenings are positive, some are negative, but the common feature among them all is the inability of one to control one's existence. The novel also deals with the idea of chance somewhat differently from other instances in which it appears prominently in Conrad's works. In *Under Western Eyes* or "Falk" or "The Duel," chance negatively affects the lives of Razumov, D'Hubert, and the unnamed narrator of "Falk." By contrast, in "A Smile of Fortune," chance affects the protagonist quite positively. In *Chance*, however, numerous examples of chance appear in the lives of the characters, some positive and some negative. In other words, it is in this novel that Conrad most extensively investigates the workings of chance in the lives of human beings, and although the novel ends happily (unlike most of Conrad's works), Conrad implies that it might just as easily have ended otherwise because in a world in which one has no control over one's existence, one can also never predict its outcome. As a result, *Chance* is one of the more interesting statements on the nature of the universe and the nature of human existence because despite its bright ending, the novel's underlying philosophy remains as dark as the bleakest of Conrad's other works.

Victory

Victory was Conrad's first novel after the commercial success of *Chance*, and it benefited from that success. The novel is about Alex Heyst, a solitary and philosophically skeptical man, who lives essentially alone on an island and is suddenly drawn out of his solitary existence when one day he travels with Captain Davidson, a ship owner, to the mainland. While Davidson is off for several weeks, Heyst stays at Schomberg's hotel and while there meets Lena, a violinist in a touring orchestra. Sensing her plight in such an existence, Heyst convinces her to run away with him. Schomberg, who had designs upon Lena himself, is angry. About this time, a Mr. Jones arrives with an assistant, Martin Ricardo, and a servant, Pedro. Jones soon intimidates Schomberg and sets up a gambling operation. Wishing to rid himself of the trio and get back at Heyst at the same time, Schomberg tells Jones about Heyst and claims that Heyst has a store of wealth on his island. Jones decides to travel to Heyst's island and arrives there with his men nearly dead from thirst. After recovering, Ricardo tries to attack Lena, but she fights him off. Seeing this incident, Heyst's servant Wang runs off in fear and takes Heyst's only gun with him. Heyst senses his danger and takes Lena to a mountain barrier that had been erected by the Alfuro people to keep civilization out and tries to get Wang, who has fled there, to let Lena pass among them, but Wang refuses, whereupon Heyst and Lena are forced to return to Heyst's dwelling. Shortly after returning, Ricardo informs Heyst that Mr. Jones wants to meet with him. Meanwhile, Ricardo eats dinner with Lena, who is able to get his dagger away from him. At that moment, Heyst and Jones return, and Jones, thinking Ricardo has betrayed him, shoots at Ricardo. The bullet grazes Ricardo and then hits Lena by mistake, killing her. Davidson suddenly arrives, and Wang, who has also returned, shoots Pedro. Jones then succeeds in shooting Ricardo, after which Jones, looking for their boat, which Wang had set adrift, tumbles into the water and drowns. Davidson, who later recounts these final events, is unsure whether Jones fell in accidentally or deliberately drowned himself. Overcome with grief, Heyst sets fire to his dwelling, committing suicide in the process.

Perhaps no other work of Conrad's has engendered such differing responses. Many feel that the novel has the same limitations of Conrad's other late fiction; others, however, consider it to be among Conrad's best works. The truth probably lies somewhere between these two extremes. Conrad's characterization of Heyst is adept, and his investigations into the necessity of human relationships and connections harks back to some of Conrad's best work. At the same time, though, some of the difficulties Conrad had in representing romantic relationships and some of the melodramatic elements that appear in his less appreciated works also appear in *Victory*.

Despite possible flaws, though, some important issues for Conrad appear in *Victory* with greater power and more sophisticated development than they do anywhere else in Conrad's works. The most important issue that arises has to do with Heyst's relationship to the objects and individuals around him. He takes a detached stance regarding the world and seeks only to observe and not to participate. Heyst has been influenced by, or perhaps more accurately, consumed by his father's radically skeptical philosophy, which went so far as to question the very existence of reality. The result of this philosophy is that Heyst removes himself from the world, both physically and emotionally, and comes to live a hermit-like existence. He is partly drawn out of this world when he helps to save his friend Morrison's ship, and later comes out further when he rescues Lena. Nevertheless, Heyst only partially integrates himself back into the world. Only with Lena's death does he fully recognize that he has missed an opportunity to connect completely with another person and thus despairs, lamenting to Davidson, "woe to the man whose heart has not learned while young to hope, to love – and to put its trust in life!" (410). By this point, it is too late, and he commits suicide. As happens so often in Conrad's works, Heyst had placed an idea (skepticism) above human interaction and relationships, and the results are disastrous.

Related to this idea of the importance of human connection is the issue of the construction of the self. In *Victory*, Conrad investigates how others influence individual selves. Heyst is a clear example of this phenomenon in that his self seems to be largely a product of his father's ideas. Only as the novel progresses does Heyst break away from his father's philosophy and even then only to a degree. An even more striking example is Lena, who, when she first appears, seems to be almost wholly devoid of self. Between the orchestra leader, Schomberg, and others, Lena's life has been so oppressed that she exhibits little individual self, and even after she escapes with Heyst her self seems molded only in the image of Heyst's conception of her. For instance, she asks Heyst to give her a new name, saying, "it seems to me, somehow, that if you were to stop thinking of me I shouldn't be in the world at all! . . . I can only be what you think I am" (187). The result is a new self. *Victory* warns of allowing the self to be subsumed as opposed to developing a fully formed self. If Marlow in "Heart of Darkness" is correct when he says that the most one can hope for out of life is some knowledge of oneself (150), then *Victory* demonstrates the grave consequences that occur when one fails to gain that knowledge until it is too late.

In addition to the importance of human connections and proper constructions of the self, human interaction in *Victory* also concerns the ideas of isolation and solidarity that appear in so many of Conrad's works. Heyst's skepticism leads to his profound isolation from other human beings, not only physically but also spiritually. His plight becomes a metaphor for humanity in the modern world. For Conrad, with the disappearance of transcendental truths, doubts concerning the existence of God, increased mechanization and industrialization, and the transient nature of the lives of so many people, one is utterly alone in the universe. Conrad suggests that only through solidarity with other human beings can one escape this ultimate isolation. As was true in Conrad's other works, however, this communion with others is only tentative and ephemeral. Lena's entrance into Heyst's life dramatically alters his isolated existence, but the connection is too short and comes too late.

Nevertheless, solidarity, though brief and fragile, is the only means to survive physically and psychologically and the only way to escape the alienation of the modern world.

Within the Tides

Within the Tides is a collection of stories that most commentators have not valued very highly. Written largely during the writing of *Victory*, and sometimes bearing some similarities with that novel, these stories generally lack its sophistication. The most interesting feature of this collection is that all of the stories introduce some kind of narrative innovation.

The first story in this collection is "The Planter of Malata." Geoffrey Renouard, the planter of the title, has just come from his isolated silk plantation on Malata, to a "great colonial city" (3), probably Sydney, Australia, where he meets Felicia Moorsam, who, in the company of relatives, has come in search of her fiancé Arthur, who has been disgraced in a financial scandal in England. In the face of that scandal, Arthur fled, though professing his innocence, and in the interim, his name has been cleared. As it turns out, unbeknownst to Renouard, Arthur has been working as Renouard's assistant under the name of Walter. Shortly before Renouard left Malata, Arthur died, but Renouard fails to mention that his assistant had died, and once it becomes known that Walter is actually Arthur, Renouard decides to say nothing because he has fallen in love with Felicia and can spend more time with her if she remains looking for Arthur. Renouard convinces the Moorsams to return to Malata with him to find Arthur, but lets on that Arthur is away. Renouard finally confesses his deception as well as his love for Felicia, who rejects him. Left alone on the island, he dismisses his workers, and when Renouard's friend the newspaper editor arrives a month later, he finds only Renouard's clothes on the beach, suggesting that Renouard swam out to sea, drowning himself.

What strengths the tale has lie largely in its having been written during the writing of *Victory*, for the story's greatest strength is in the characterization of Renouard. Renouard, like Heyst in *Victory*, has tried to remove himself from the rest of humanity, working largely in isolation and divorced from close ties with others. What he discovers, again like Heyst, is that such a life is bleak and without meaning. Ironically, Renouard's reintroduction into the world of human ties proves to be his undoing. Renouard completely romanticizes Felicia and is unable to see her for the shallow person she is. As a result, when she rejects him, he despairs. Nevertheless, his return from human isolation is something of a victory. His life has attained a kind of meaning whereas before it was devoid of any. In contrast to Renouard, throughout the story, Felicia remains detached from human connections. Unlike Renouard who has been isolated on his plantation, Felicia is constantly in social situations, but she has no true connections with other people. Even her search for Arthur has less to do with the connection between them than with Felicia's own conception of herself as rescuing Arthur from his disgrace. Furthermore, she rejects both Arthur and Renouard, first when she refuses to believe Arthur's protests of innocence during the scandal and second when she rejects Renouard's declaration of love. While Renouard has been rejected and is physically dead at the end of the story, at least he had managed to bring himself back into the world of human relations. Felicia, however, remains detached and thus spiritually dead at the story's conclusion.

The other point of interest regarding "The Planter of Malata" has to do with the consistent juxtaposition of Realism and Romanticism in the story. Both Renouard and Felicia represent the Romantic, each viewing the world through such lenses, while the newspaper editor in particular and the rest of the characters represent the Realistic world. This juxtaposition is most apparent in the mundane activities in which the various characters engage while Renouard's Romantic passions swirl in his mind. Similarly, the editor's steadfast inability to conceive of Renouard's Romantic suicide further solidifies the contrast between these two seemingly mutually exclusive worlds. Conrad, as he does so often, seems to be pointing out the limitations of both ways of looking at the world.

"The Partner" is certainly one of the most unusual and interesting works in the Conrad canon. The story has typically been dismissed as a potboiler with little redeeming value, but such a view underestimates it. Without doubt, the story's plot has little to recommend it. Cloete is an American confidence man, who tries to get his partner, George Dunbar, to arrange the wreck of their ship in order to collect the insurance money so that they can invest it in a lumbago pills business. Cloete hires Stafford to arrange the wreck, but the plot goes awry when Stafford first tries to blackmail Cloete for more money and then when he kills the ship's captain, Harry Dunbar, George's brother, while trying to rob him. The result is that everyone assumes that the captain committed suicide, which causes his widow to go insane, and the insurance money that was to have gone to Harry goes to his widow instead and hence is never invested in the lumbago pills business. The money that goes to George ends up insufficient for the investment, and Cloete, disappointed at his missed opportunity, returns to America.

However, the narrative method has much to recommend it, unlike the mundane plot. Certainly the most sophisticated and interesting of the narrative methodologies employed in this collection, in many ways it harks back to techniques Conrad had employed much earlier in his career. The information in the story comes through a variety of sources and hence, like "Heart of Darkness," *Lord Jim*, and other works, the certainty of the information in "The Partner" comes into question, that is various differing views of the events arise, thereby calling into question any single, objective account. Linked to the multiple views is the frame narrative that Conrad employs. Unlike the Marlow narratives, for example, the frame in this story is highly interactive. In other words, although the tale is told by the stevedore, the unnamed writer character often interrupts, comments, and otherwise intrudes upon the stevedore's tale. The primary effect of this interactive frame narration is to contrast the stevedore's view of the events with those of the writer. Furthermore, the two characters serve to comment on the idea of the writer and the writer's public. Conrad satirizes the writer of popular fiction, who appears in the character of the writer in the story. The writer is unable to appreciate the significance of what he hears, and the stevedore, who seems to bear some striking similarities to Conrad himself, recognizes the shallowness of the writer. In this way, Conrad is able to criticize both the popular writer and the popular reading public, which, like the shallow writer in "The Partner," is unable to recognize significant moral and psychological dramas – like those Conrad himself wrote.

Even more than the other stories in this volume, "The Inn of the Two Witches" has been dismissed as having no literary value. The plot is certainly melodramatic and gothic, but there are interesting aspects of the story nonetheless. Set in Spain, Edgar Byrne goes off in search of a fellow shipmate, Tom Corbin, and comes upon an inn where Tom had stayed. The inn is inhabited by what Byrne terms two witches and a demon woman. After going to his room, he believes he hears Tom's voice warning him to be careful. He finally gets up from bed and forces open a wardrobe, finding Tom's dead body inside. While mourning the loss of his friend and trying to discover how he had died, Byrne moves the body to the bed. Unable to discover the cause of Tom's death and distraught by grief and fright, Byrne suddenly notices the canopy of the bed dropping down, smothering Tom's body. At that moment, Byrne hears voices below and looks outside. Thinking a mob has come to kill him, he rushes out at them and is knocked senseless. It turns out that the mob was actually a group of men under the command of Gonzales, a man friendly toward Byrne, who was impatient to learn the fate of Byrne and

Corbin and had come in search of them. Byrne wakes up to learn that the three women and an accomplice have been executed.

As is true of all of the stories in *Within the Tides*, the narrative construction of "The Inn of the Two Witches" is of interest. The story is a frame narrative in the form of a "found" manuscript. An unnamed frame narrator purportedly finds a manuscript that was written by Byrne some forty years after the events occurred. Furthermore, Byrne obtains some of the information about the events in the story from other individuals. As a result, the events and views on those events are filtered through a variety of sources, each with varying perspectives. The clearest distinctions occur in the differing views of the frame narrator and that of Byrne, but even Byrne himself, chronicling the events so many years after the fact, betrays a different perspective from that which he had at the time the events occurred. All of this brings up, as it did in "The Partner," the relativity and subjectivity of the views that are narrated. In addition to the narrative technique, the story has further interest in the emotions Byrne exhibits; the almost wholly paralyzing fear Byrne feels is well drawn by Conrad, as is Byrne's grief at his friend's death. Although this story's literary quality will never be confused with that of "The Secret Sharer," "The Inn of the Two Witches" nevertheless warrants more than its usual cursory dismissal.

"Because of the Dollars" closes this collection and was originally envisioned as part of *Victory*. Davidson runs into Laughing Anne, a former prostitute he once knew. After a rash of men loving and leaving her, she has taken up with Bamtz, a seedy character, who is supposed to have reformed and become a small-time rattan trader in an isolated region of the Malay Archipelago. Out of compassion for Anne and her son Tony, Davidson includes Bamtz on his regular trading run. The government is changing currency and requiring people to exchange all of their old currency. Davidson is entrusted with collecting the money and makes the mistake of mentioning it within earshot of three ruffians, who then go to Bamtz and lie in wait for Davidson, intending to kill him and steal the money. One is a Frenchman without hands, who has forced Anne to tie a weight to one of his stumps. Anne warns Davidson, and when the men try to surprise him he is ready for them. Realizing that they have been betrayed, the Frenchman bludgeons Anne to death. Davidson succeeds in killing him, but the others flee, including Bamtz, who has been a reluctant accomplice. Only the boy is left, whom Davidson then takes home. When his wife learns of Anne's past, however, she believes Tony to be Davidson and Anne's son and promptly leaves Davidson.

Like the other stories in *Within the Tides*, "Because of the Dollars" has usually been considered of little literary merit. Also like the other stories, the tale employs a narrative methodology that is not straightforward. The story proceeds by way of a frame narrative, resulting in multiple perspectives – although interestingly the unnamed narrator to whom Hollis relates his tale appears to make no real judgments regarding what he hears. This is a departure from Conrad's usual practice of playing off the frame narrator's views against those of other characters and also against those of the reader. Nevertheless, Hollis provides strong opinions about what he relates, opinions that may often run counter to those of the reader. The most interesting aspect of the story, though, may be the view of goodness that appears. Davidson is presented as a "good" person, as is Anne. The disasters that occur in the story, with the exception of Davidson's conversation about the dollars being overheard, result from Davidson's goodness. The same is true of Anne's fate; her death results from her goodness in trying to save Davidson's life. It seems that Conrad may be suggesting rather pessimistically that being good is a liability in the world. Both Anne's and Davidson's goodness certainly prove to be liabilities, making the two vulnerable to the negative actions of others. On the other hand, despite the tragedies that both endure, they are clearly the most admirable characters in the story, certainly far more so than Davidson's wife, who despite her social respectability (in contrast to Anne's) appears not so very much better than Bamtz and the ruffians who plan to rob and kill Davidson. Perhaps Conrad suggests that the goodness of Anne and Davidson is worth the tragedies that befall them and that goodness may in fact be its own reward.

The Shadow-Line

The Shadow-Line is unusual among Conrad's later works because whether one sees a decline in these works or a change of creative direction, *The Shadow-Line* is an anomaly. The novel has much more in common with the works of Conrad's middle period than it does with those of his later period, and it is clearly the most powerful of Conrad's later works.

The Shadow-Line is a story of initiation from apprenticeship to mastery of command, much like "The Secret Sharer," but it is also the story of crossing that shadowy line from youth into manhood. A young captain receives his first command, but his initial voyage as captain is beset with difficulties. Almost all of the ship's crew fall ill, and to make matters worse the captain discovers that his predecessor had sold the ship's stock of quinine and replaced it with a worthless powder. Under ordinary circumstances, this development would not have been so dangerous, but in this case the ship is caught in a dead calm and can make no progress. The narrator notes, "The Island of Koh-ring . . . seemed to be the centre of the fatal circle. It seemed impossible to get away from it. Day after day it remained in sight" (84). As a result, their predicament becomes dire, and in the midst of this crisis the young captain, again like the protagonist of "The Secret Sharer," wonders about his abilities to live up to the expectations of command: "I always suspected that I might be no good" (107). In the end, however, he proves to be up to the task, and with the help of his ailing crew and a much-needed break in the weather is able to bring the ship safely into port without loss of life or damage to the ship. To do so, though, the captain and the crew must learn to cooperate and rely on one another. As happens in *The Nigger of the "Narcissus"* and "Typhoon," cooperation among the men is crucial to their continued survival, and lack of it threatens their very existence. Despite their illness, the various crew members attend to their duties as soon as they can get themselves out of their sick beds. They all work together in trying to survive the voyage, and while their actions demonstrate the importance of cooperation, the actions of the ship's previous captain demonstrate the danger of its lack. Mr. Burns, the ship's Chief Mate, says of the previous captain:

> He never meant her [the ship] to see home again. He wouldn't write to his owners, he never wrote to his old wife either – he wasn't going to. He had made up his mind to cut adrift from everything. That's what it was. He didn't care for business, or freights, or for making a passage – or anything. He meant to have gone wandering about the world till he lost her with all hands. (61–2)

The previous captain's actions threaten the ship and its crew and represent a breach in the social contract that exists between captain and crew. The young captain comments that the previous captain's actions were "a complete act of treason, the betrayal of a tradition which seemed to [the young captain] as imperative as any guide on earth could be" (62). The previous captain's actions, however, have even greater repercussions because they not only affect those who served under him but also those who serve under his successor, because selling the ship's quinine turns an uncomfortable situation into a deadly one, and it is only through the efforts of the crew and the luck of the weather change that they survive their ordeal. In bringing about the ship's safety, Ransome, the ship's cook, is particularly important. He and the young captain are the only crew members who do not fall ill. Ransome has a heart condition, but despite the danger of his condition and despite the fact that death constantly faces him, he puts all his effort into saving the ship. His actions starkly contrast with those of the ship's previous captain. The result of this voyage and of the young captain's meeting his challenges is that he crosses over that shadow line into maturity, both as a captain and as a human being.

As he does in many of his other works, Conrad also considers the larger issue of the nature of human existence in *The Shadow-Line*. On the open ocean, the men are cut off from civilization and the safety of the shore. There are no external restraints upon them, and each man aboard must find within himself the strength and commitment to participate as a member of a community and thus accept his responsibilities to the others. All that holds their community together is their obligation toward one another. During the voyage, their lives are in danger, and their precarious hold on life is analogous to that of human existence in general. Their lives are saved in part through their cooperation and efforts, but the larger part of their fate results from the chance change of weather. Both the origin and disappearance of the dead calm are mysteries. When the calm arises, the narrator comments, "There was no sense in it. It fitted neither with the season of the year, nor with the secular experience of seamen as recorded in books, nor with the aspect of the sky" (87). The calm disappears just as mysteriously. In these events, Conrad emphasizes the tenuous nature of human existence and the powerful role of fate in it.

The Arrow of Gold

While in the case of *Victory*, no other book of Conrad's has elicited such a mixed reaction, in the case of *The Arrow of Gold*, no other book of Conrad's has evoked such strong dissatisfaction. Although the novel has its defenders, even its defenders rarely attempt to make a case for it being worthy of most of Conrad's other works. In composing the novel, Conrad first began dictating a majority of the material. The result was a much easier time composing than was usual for Conrad, but at the same time perhaps a commensurate sacrifice in the quality of the final product followed. Most critics would probably agree that the painstaking, laborious method of composition by hand that Conrad typically employed tended to result in better writing.

The novel begins with Monsieur George meeting Captain Blunt and Mr. Mills, both Carlist supporters. They discuss a certain Doña Rita, another Carlist supporter. Later, Mills brings George to meet Rita. George then becomes involved in gunrunning for the Carlists, engaging in several runs during the course of the novel. Eventually, George falls in love with Rita and learns that Blunt wishes to marry her. In the end, Rita refuses Blunt, and shortly thereafter George declares his love for her but is left uncertain about her feelings toward him. Later, after his nearly disastrous gunrunning expedition, when George returns to Marseilles, he is instructed to meet a man named Ortega. George soon discovers that Ortega is unstable and obsessed with Rita. George takes him back to his lodgings, not knowing that Rita is there. When Ortega realizes that Rita is there, he tries to break into her room. Before he succeeds, he accidentally wounds himself and Rita and George escape. The two spend an idyllic six months together, after which George comes back to Marseilles for a short business trip and learns that Blunt has been defaming him. This results in a duel in which George is wounded. When he finally recovers, George finds that Rita has disappeared, presumably out of concern that her relationship with George is dangerous to him.

Although the novel has been roundly criticized, there are nevertheless some interesting aspects worth noting. The narrative methodology in some ways harks back to Conrad's earlier method of presenting material from differing perspectives. *The Arrow of Gold* employs multiple perspectives on events and individuals, although in a less sophisticated manner than "Heart of Darkness," *Lord Jim*, or *Chance*, for example. There is a frame narrator of sorts, who appears in the opening and concluding notes, and edits George's account of some of the events of his youth. Furthermore, several characters, particularly during the early part of the novel, present differing perspectives on Rita; later in the novel, other characters, such as Ortega, Rita's sister Therese, and Blunt's mother, present their views of Rita, and finally Rita herself relates part of her history to George. The result is a variety of perspectives on events and particularly on Rita. Unlike in some of Conrad's earlier works, however, the multiplicity of perspectives is not as sustained nor as emphasized, although it does demonstrate how much subjectivity influences how something appears. Furthermore, the three main views represented in the novel, the editor's view, George's mature view, and George's youthful view, provide for interesting contrasts in perspective and interpretation.

A more important point of interest has to do with issues of gender politics. In addition to the differing views of Rita presented by the various characters, the representation of Rita as an object of desire and as a fallen woman presents interesting questions regarding the role of women in Western society of the time. Although she is portrayed as a strong woman, Rita has clearly been victimized at various times during her life. Even from her position of power, wealth, and admiration, her actions and activities are circumscribed within the boundaries of what society will allow her as a woman. In addition, the danger she experiences results almost solely from the fact that she is only an object of male desire. Despite her significant role in the Carlist cause, the men consider her value almost exclusively to be that of a desirable woman: they all desire her and objectify her within those terms. The result is a psychologically damaged woman who can find no lasting peace in her life. Nevertheless, she still exhibits strength in refusing to become the object of male possession, as she alternately rejects the Carlist would-be king, Blunt, Ortega, and even George, and although she is willing to live with George for a time, she ultimately chooses to leave him and thereby remains in full possession of her self.

The Rover

The Rover was Conrad's last completed novel. It begins with Jean Peyrol returning to France after many years away as a rover on the seas. While away, the French Revolution has occurred and is now on its wane. Peyrol wanders off from Toulon to the place of his childhood and finds lodging at a farmhouse on a peninsula. The farmhouse was formally owned by Royalists who lost their lives in the revolution and is now inhabited by Arlette, their daughter, her aunt Catherine, and Scevola Bron, a fervent Jacobite, who gave full vent to his bloodthirsty ways during the revolution. Arlette has been traumatized by the deaths of her parents and by witnessing so much carnage during the revolution. Eight years pass, and Peyrol has become fully acclimated to life on the farm. Meanwhile, Napoleon has come to power, and the French are at war with the British, who are trying to blockade the port of Toulon. An English ship patrols the waters outside the port, and Lieutenant Réal is sent to the farmhouse to investigate the ship's activities. He soon becomes friendly with Peyrol and ultimately falls in love with Arlette. The French develop a plan to deceive the English: Réal is to carry false documents about the deployment of French forces and then allow himself to be caught by the English. Scevola, who recognizes Réal as a rival for Arlette, sets out to kill him with a pitchfork but is captured in the hold of Peyrol's boat. Just before Réal is to set sail on his mission, Peyrol sends him back to the farmhouse on a pretext and then sets off in his place. Cleverly leading the English on, Peyrol eventually allows himself to be caught. Peyrol, Scevola, and Michel, Peyrol's friend and helper, are shot during their mock escape, but Peyrol is successful in his mission, as the documents fall into the hands of the

English. The novel ends some years after Peyrol's death with Arlette and Réal married and affectionately discussing Peyrol.

In many ways, *The Rover* is a return for Conrad. For a number of years, he had planned to write about the Napoleonic period of France, but until *The Rover* he had written only two stories using that setting ("The Duel" and "The Warrior's Soul"). *The Rover* and the unfinished *Suspense* were the continuation of his interest in the period. In addition to the Napoleonic setting, Conrad also returns to the sea and to a number of issues that populated his earlier fiction. Peyrol embodies a number of the qualities that Conrad infused into his most admirable characters from his sea fiction. Peyrol is self-sufficient, eminently proficient in his profession, and a man who can be relied upon to carry his weight in a crisis. He also embodies the concept of solidarity in that despite having been away from France since he was a boy, when he returns, something of an outlaw and largely indifferent to politics, he nevertheless develops a connection with the land and with his country, in the end sacrificing his life for the better good of France and for the future of Arlette and Réal.

In addition to solidarity, Conrad also turns his attention once again to revolutionary politics, as they are embodied in the character of Scevola as well as in the French Revolution itself. As was true of Conrad's previous political writings that dealt with revolutionary politics, again in *The Rover* Conrad exhibits his profound skepticism of both revolutionary and established politics. Clearly, Scevola is presented as unsympathetically as Nikita in *Under Western Eyes* or the Professor in *The Secret Agent*. In fact, Scevola seems to embody the worst of both in his bloodthirsty desires and precarious grip on sanity. At the same time, though, Peyrol's loyalty to France seems to be more of a connection to the land and the general concept of the nation of France than to the actual ruling government, toward which Peyrol exhibits the same skepticism as he does toward Scevola's political views.

There also appears to be a good deal of Conrad himself in the character of Peyrol. Roughly the same age as Conrad when he was writing the novel, Peyrol appears to exhibit some of the same attitudes as Conrad. Returning to his homeland after many years away and removed from the political upheavals in the interim, Peyrol finds himself drawn back to France much the way Conrad was later in his life, particularly after his visit to Poland in 1914. Prior to that time, Conrad took little public interest in the affairs in Poland in fact expressing a good deal of pessimism toward both the future prospects of Poland and toward the political activism of Polish patriots, viewing such actions as hopelessly doomed to failure. After Conrad's visit, he took a much more active role in the affairs of Poland, writing tracts condemning European aggression toward Poland and supporting Polish independence, as well as actively lobbying the British public and government on behalf of Poland. In many ways, the careers of Peyrol and his author parallel one another.

Similarly, Peyrol makes a choice late in the novel to sacrifice his life not just for his community and country but also for the rising generation. His affection for Arlette causes him to replace Réal with himself on the suicide mission to outwit the English. In this way, he passes on to Réal and Arlette a future together, as they build their lives and the life of France. With his final action, Peyrol is passing the baton to the next generation, going out of this life having lived a full life as a productive member of society at the very end. Conrad's letters, as well as his spotty work on *Suspense*, suggest that he felt somewhat like Peyrol. He frequently expressed great fatigue and the feeling that he was coming to the end of his life, the difference being perhaps that the masterwork that Conrad envisioned for *Suspense* remained unfulfilled at the time of his death.

The Rover has been much neglected, and this has been an oversight. If the novel lacks the power and sophistication of some of Conrad's other work, it still has much that is of merit. The characterization of Peyrol as well as Conrad's revisiting some of his most powerful themes are a welcome return in this the last of his completed fictional works.

Tales of Hearsay

This collection of stories was published posthumously and collected several stories that had previously appeared only in magazine form. The name of the volume was apparently one that Conrad himself had considered for a collection of stories, and the volume was introduced by Conrad's long-time friend R. B. Cunninghame Graham. Whether Conrad would have included all of the stories is questionable. Jessie Conrad believed that Conrad would not have.

"The Black Mate" is the slightest story in this collection and has engendered far more discussion as a result of the debate over its origins than over its literary merits. Conrad claimed to have begun the story in the 1880s in order to submit it to a magazine competition. Jessie Conrad, however, said that she gave Conrad the idea for the story, which would make its origins much later. If the story had been begun when Conrad claimed it to have been, it, rather than *Almayer's Folly*, would mark the beginning of Conrad's literary career. As to the story itself, the main character, Bunter, dyes his prematurely white hair in order to get a job as a mate. During the ensuing voyage, though, his remaining dye is destroyed during a storm. The ship's captain, a self-righteous man, looks down on Bunter. He also believes strongly in spirits. Knowing that his white hair will soon begin to show through, Bunter tricks the captain by claiming he has seen a ghost, which turns his hair white.

As to the story's literary merit, most commentators would not consider it to be a particularly strong story, and it would be difficult to dispute such an evaluation. There are, however, a few points worth noting. Although the issues of isolation and honorable behavior remain largely uninvestigated in the story, they do appear. Bunter's need to struggle in isolation with the fear that his deception will be uncovered evokes, on a much lesser scale, images of similar psychological struggles in other Conrad characters. Finally, Conrad's suspicion of religious sensibility and scorn of hypocrisy (in the form of Bunter's captain) run throughout the story and remind one of similar characters sprinkled throughout so many of Conrad's other works. Nevertheless, unlike Conrad's best works, such issues are not the story's main focus but merely ancillary.

"Prince Roman" is Conrad's most unusual fictional work. Essentially devoid of irony, it presents a revolutionary figure in a positive light, directly engages a Polish topic, and sympathetically portrays a character in a happy position at the story's close. Recently happily married, Prince Roman is devastated when his young wife suddenly dies. He gives up his position in the Russian guards, assumes an alias, and joins the Polish insurgent forces. He is later captured and brought to trial, where he is recognized. A sympathetic judge, wanting to spare him, suggests that grief caused Prince Roman to follow the path he did, but the Prince instead states that he acted out of conviction and thus receives a twenty-five year sentence to Siberia. After completing his sentence, he returns home and continues to act for the benefit of his people.

Both laudatory and patriotic, the story unequivocally sympathizes with the patriotic self-sacrifice of Prince Roman, further presenting him in a favorable light through his inexhaustible community service despite his physical limitations. The story also appears to be based not only on the experience of an actual historical figure but also on Conrad's own experience as a young boy when he is supposed to have met Prince Roman himself. Perhaps, though, the most interesting aspect of the story from a literary perspective is the comment that occurs toward the end of the story in which we learn that the prince's daughter and son-in-law fail to recognize the prince's merits, which Conrad clearly admires and seems to expect that the reader will also admire. The daughter and son-in-law dismiss the prince, ascribing to him the fault of being "guided too much by mere sentiment" (55). In this incident, Conrad criticizes the couple, who directly reap the benefit of their wealth from Prince Roman's actions of sentiment but fail to appreciate those same actions.

"The Warrior's Soul" is one of Conrad's better late stories. Another of his works set in Napoleonic France, the story begins at the outbreak of hostilities between France and Russia. De Castel, a French officer, warns his friend Tomassov, a Russian officer living in France at the time, that war has been declared, and thus Tomassov eludes capture. Later, during the retreat from Napoleon's disastrous Russian campaign, Tomassov's regiment captures some retreating French soldiers. Among them is de Castel, who has lost all faith and courage and asks Tomassov to kill him and thus repay the debt he owes to de Castel. Tomassov unwillingly obliges him. Like *The Rover*, "The Warrior's Soul" harks back to some of Conrad's earliest works as it investigates the moral and psychological conflict of Tomassov. Tomassov is forced to choose between what he feels to be morally right and what he feels to be honorably right. His choice is not enviable, and the tension between Tomassov's choice of moralities is what gives the story its power.

In addition to the story's psychological power, the circumstances of its writing are also of interest. Written during the First World War, the devastation of war in the story is eerily similar to that in the trenches in Europe at the time. Further emphasizing the senselessness of war is the contrast between the two worlds in the story, that of French society before the war begins and of Russian battlefields after. The same men who enjoyed one another's company before the war become adversaries once it begins, the change in their relationship coming from their leaders not from the men. Left to themselves, the men never would have initiated such a conflict. As Conrad suggests elsewhere, it is always the individuals who are caught between the larger political forces.

"The Tale" is a story that returns to some of Conrad's earlier works in that it depicts the psychological struggles of a captain, who suspecting a ship of trafficking with the enemy during World War I, deliberately gives the captain of that ship incorrect directions, believing that those directions will be ignored because the ship is aware of the region through its illegal actions. The ship, however, follows the captain's instructions exactly and sinks, killing all aboard. The significance of this tale lies in several areas. First, the captain's inability to assess conclusively whether the other ship was trafficking with the enemy gives the story its peculiar power. The captain does not know whether he was right or wrong and hence feels guilty that he may have sent innocent men to their deaths. What makes this situation particularly poignant is that the captain can never know for sure and thus can never escape his feelings of guilt. Linked to the captain's guilt is Conrad's implicit commentary on the nature of war. In this story, Conrad shows how the exigencies of war blur the boundaries between right and wrong and cause all involved to act counter to moral behavior because even if the captain is correct about the activities of the other ship the sentence he pronounces upon its men is not one a moral person can easily accept. Finally, the narrative method of this story has attracted much attention. Both the physical fog that appears in the story, representing the moral fog that engulfs the captain's actions, and the multiple frame technique reveal Conrad's last foray into formal experimentation and narrative complexity. And as is so often true in Conrad's works, the complexity of the narrative mirrors the moral, psychological, and epistemological complexities the story investigates.

Suspense

Suspense remained incomplete at the time of Conrad's death and was published posthumously in 1925. The novel is set primarily in Genoa in 1815, during the suspense-filled time just before Napoleon returned to France from his exile on Elba. It is the story of a young man, Cosmo Latham, who has been traveling and come to Genoa to visit the Marquis d'Armand and his daughter Adèle, the Countess de Montevesso. The Marquis and his family were friends of Latham's father, Sir Charles Latham, and lived at Latham Hall for a time after escaping from France during the French Revolution. Having fled for their lives, the Marquis and his family had arrived in England impoverished. In order to provide security for her family, Adèle later married the wealthy but uncultured Count de Montevesso, who is many years her senior.

Shortly after the novel opens, Latham goes for a walk to a local tower and encounters and aids a man (Attilio), who is engaged in passing secret documents. Latham then returns to his inn and the following day pays a visit to Adèle and her father, whom he has not seen for some ten years. During the course of his visit, Latham learns the sad story of Adèle's history with her husband, who has subjected her to his fits of jealousy, calumny, and suspicion. Latham is clearly attracted to Adèle, and after he returns to his inn there is some suggestion that Adèle's husband may be seeking to assassinate Latham out of jealousy. The next day, after spending the entire day writing a letter to his sister, Latham suddenly rushes out of the inn to go for a walk down by the port. While there, Latham again encounters Attilio, who is being sought by the authorities. Attilio hides some documents in Latham's hat and runs off just before the authorities arrive and arrest Latham. Latham discovers the documents only when he puts his hat on. Shortly afterwards, Latham is to be transported across the harbor and incarcerated. On the way, Attilio ambushes the transport boat, subduing the guards and rescuing

Latham. Attilio and Latham then elude the authorities in the immediate vicinity, and the book concludes with Latham and Attilio rowing away from Genoa to escape further pursuit.

It is difficult to know what the novel might have become had Conrad lived to complete it. He had conceived of the novel perhaps as early as 1902 but put off its writing for many years. Conrad had high hopes for *Suspense*, envisioning it as a masterwork. What he left behind, however, falls far short of that goal. Most commentators have generally dismissed the novel as of no real consequence, and there is much justification for such opinions. At the same time, though, there is some promise in this unfinished novel. Conrad does an excellent job of evoking the atmosphere of fear, intrigue, suspicion, and of course suspense that filled the air at that time. The theme of youth moving into adulthood also appears to have been one of the ideas that Conrad had planned to pursue. In addition, there is the hint of an incest theme in the novel with the suggestion that Latham's father also may have fathered Adèle. Perhaps the most promising idea evoked in *Suspense*, however, is that represented by Adèle's situation. Her poignant story of self-sacrifice for her family and the persecution she endures at the hands of her husband might have been, if expanded upon, a powerful statement regarding the plight of women in the world and the all-too-common need for women to sacrifice happiness for security, as well as their powerless position in abusive relationships, a plight that was as true in the time the novel was written as it was in the time it was set.

Conrad's only other fictional work was the novel fragment *The Sisters* – a mere thirty-nine pages in manuscript. Conrad began this work in 1895 and abandoned it shortly thereafter. Unlike so many of the other works he set aside, Conrad never returned to *The Sisters* and he appears to have never intended to finish it. The posthumous publication of *The Sisters* in 1928 ends the literary career of one of the most important and unique authors of the twentieth century. Consistently in the forefront of literary ideas and innovation, Conrad would become one of the most influential authors of his time.

Chapter 6

Conrad criticism

In this chapter, I will discuss the critical reception of Conrad's works both at the time he was writing and afterwards. My goal is to present a history of the criticism and in the process discuss important studies of Conrad's works and identify crucial debates surrounding them. I will look at some of the early commentaries on Conrad's works, as well as Conrad's movement from canonical status to a state of disfavor to his reinstatement as a canonical writer. I will then follow his critical reception until the present.

During Conrad's lifetime, the reviews of his fiction were generally quite favorable. In fact, for some of his works the critical reception was even more favorable then than it is now. Given the number of commentaries on Conrad's work, it would be impossible to address them all. Even the book-length studies are too numerous to consider all of them, and so I have been forced to leave out many good commentaries. In outlining the history of Conrad criticism, I will consider those studies with which any student of Conrad's works should be familiar, along with those that have been important to the development of Conrad criticism, because of the work's high quality, because it marked an important moment in Conrad criticism, or because it initiated or continued a significant branch of Conrad criticism. In the process of this survey, I will focus largely on book-length studies since they have usually been the most important to the development of Conrad criticism. At the same time, though, I have also included those essays and book chapters that have made particularly significant contributions to Conrad criticism.

Several book-length studies of Conrad's life and works were written during his lifetime. Of those, only Richard Curle's *Joseph Conrad: A Study* (1914) and Wilson Follett's *Joseph Conrad: A Short Study* (1915) made significant contributions to Conrad studies. Curle's *Joseph Conrad: A Study*, being the first book-length study of Conrad's work, takes up a number of the issues upon which later commentators would expand. Curle classifies Conrad as a Realistic Romanticist, and his book is important for the scholarly interest it generated in Conrad's works, for Curle's recognition of Conrad's use of irony and fixed ideas, for his recognition of the quality of Conrad's works, and for some good readings of individual works. Nevertheless, the value of Curle's book is primarily as a catalyst for later more extensive and significant discussions of many of the issues that Curle considers. In contrast, Follett's *Joseph Conrad: A Short Study* is the first truly sophisticated study of Conrad's works, particularly useful is his commentary on the issues of an indifferent universe and the need for solidarity. Follett's is certainly the best of the early books on Conrad and has been unnecessarily neglected. Although the language is somewhat overblown, Follett clearly identifies the irrational and indifferent universe in which Conrad's characters exist. He also shows a continuity among Conrad's works and consistently identifies crucial passages and issues arising in these works.

Among the shorter commentaries that appeared during this time, several are worth mentioning because they all anticipate important debates in Conrad studies. Grace Isabel Colbron, in "Joseph Conrad's Women," which appeared in the January 1914 issue of *The Bookman*, recognizes many of the limitations of the female characters in Conrad's works and begins the important discussion of women in Conrad's works long before it would become a prominent area of Conrad criticism. Henry James, in his essay "The Younger Generation: Part II," which appeared in the *Times Literary Supplement* on April 2, 1914, addresses the issue of the quality of Conrad's later works. James's was one of the few voices to express reservations about Conrad's *Chance* when he suggested that the book privileges form over content, an opinion that would later be echoed by many others. Similarly, in "Mr. Conrad: A Conversation," which appeared in *Nation & Athenæum* on September 1, 1923 and in a review published in the *Times Literary Supplement* on July 1, 1920, Virginia Woolf questions the quality of *The Arrow of Gold* and *The Rescue*; like James, Woolf would be one of the few dissenting voices in the general atmosphere of praise surrounding Conrad's later works, as she anticipated subsequent criticism of these novels. Finally, on a broader level, in a review of Conrad's essay collection, *Notes on Life and Letters* that appeared in *Nation & Athenæum* on March 19, 1921, E. M. Forster took the opportunity to remark on Conrad's works as a whole, famously commenting that Conrad "is misty in the middle as well as at the edges, that the secret casket of his genius contains a vapour rather than a jewel." This evaluation has served as the starting point for much commentary since.

Immediately following Conrad's death, a variety of commentaries appeared, several of which are worth noting. Ford Madox Ford's *Joseph Conrad: A Personal Remembrance* (1924) at times provides useful commentary on Conrad's works, method of composition, and theory of literature. Ford's book, however, is most useful when corroborated by other documentation. One must always be skeptical in accepting Ford's assertions because the book has been roundly criticized for historical and biographical inaccuracies. Similarly, Jessie Conrad's *Joseph Conrad as I Knew Him* (1926) provides some useful and interesting biographical information, but the fact that some of her information runs counter to established facts suggests that this book, too, must be studied with some skepticism. The last important biographical work to appear during this time was G. Jean-Aubry's *Joseph Conrad: Life and Letters* (1927), a biography and collection of letters integrated into the biographical material. Long a definitive source for Conrad's biography and correspondence, it has now been largely superseded.

Not long after Conrad's death, opinions about his works began to shift dramatically. By 1930, both Richard Curle and Granville Hicks noted a decline in Conrad's reputation. In his essay "Conrad and the Younger Generation," which appeared in the January 1930 issue of *Nineteenth Century*, Curle remarked that the younger generation regarded Conrad "as an exotic 'spirit,' rather than as a serious novelist." Similarly, Hicks, in his article, "Conrad after Five Years," published in the *New Republic* on January 8, 1930, suggested that Conrad's reputation was shrinking because he was not a sociological novelist and was perceived to be a writer of Romance and adventure rather than the philosophical novelist that he was. Nevertheless, several worthwhile books appeared during the 1930s. In *The Twentieth Century Novel: Studies in Technique* (1931), Joseph Warren Beach includes a chapter on Conrad's literary technique, presenting the first extended and intelligent discussion of Conrad's Impressionism. In the area of biography, Gustav Morf's *The Polish Heritage of Joseph Conrad* (1930) deals with biographical issues, particularly Conrad's Polish heritage, and it was the first early study of Conrad with staying power. Good as Follett's book is, it has fallen into relative obscurity. In contrast, Morf's book is still useful, although it has been overshadowed by more recent work, particularly that of Zdzisław Najder. Morf's was the first detailed account of Conrad's Polish background and the first clear demonstration of the importance of that background on the formation of his fiction. Other commentators, such as Hugh Walpole in *Joseph Conrad* (1916) and Ernst Bendz in *Joseph Conrad: An Appreciation* (1923), had used biographical information to try to understand Conrad's works, but Morf's access to Polish materials was a significant addition to biographical criticism of Conrad's works. His readings of such writings as *Lord Jim, Nostromo,* and "Amy Foster" focus on Conrad's Polish background to interpret them. Furthermore, regardless of whether one agrees with Morf's readings, they are often well argued and have formed the basis for much later debate. Another biographical study is Jessie Conrad's *Joseph*

Conrad and His Circle (1935). A companion to her *Joseph Conrad as I Knew Him*, this book possesses the same strengths and weaknesses of her earlier book. Rather than biography, William Wallace Bancroft's *Joseph Conrad: His Philosophy of Life* (1931) is the first extended discussion of Conrad's philosophy as it appears in his works. In many ways, this book has been superseded by later discussions, but it is nevertheless worth consulting. Bancroft considers Conrad's emphasis on the moral law and particularly on the importance of human solidarity. Furthermore, his thoughtful discussion of some of Conrad's more neglected works such as "The Return" and "The Idiots" invites their further consideration. Another kind of inquiry into Conrad's thinking appears in R. L. Mégroz's *Joseph Conrad's Mind and Method* (1931). While perpetuating some of the faults of other studies of the time (too much praise and too little analysis), this book also contains some useful commentary. For instance, Mégroz is the first commentator to argue that women play a much larger role in Conrad's works than is typically perceived, a view that was almost universally overlooked until relatively recently. Similarly, Mégroz does a good job of identifying some of the plotting and narrative techniques that Conrad employs to obtain the effect he does and to represent setting and action realistically. Like several other commentaries of this time, Edward Crankshaw's *Joseph Conrad: Some Aspects of the Art of the Novel* (1936) has some interesting insights into Conrad's works, such as the contrapuntal structure in *Chance* and the idea that Conrad's works are artistic unities. In addition, Crankshaw includes extended discussions of some of Conrad's less-studied works. Crankshaw's main intent is to rescue Conrad's reputation, but he avoids the pitfall of praise without analysis that plagues so many other early commentaries. A particularly important book published around this time was John Dozier Gordon's *Joseph Conrad: The Making of a Novelist* (1940). Along with useful commentary on Conrad's works, Gordon's book is the first in-depth analysis of the history and composition process of Conrad's writings and hence is particularly useful for textual criticism of Conrad's works. This book really marks the beginning of modern criticism on Conrad.

By the late 1930s, there had been rumblings about the need to recover Conrad's reputation. M. C. Bradbrook's *Joseph Conrad, Józef Teodor Konrad Nałęcz Korzeniowski: Poland's English Genius* (1941) furthers the work begun by Crankshaw and others to re-establish Conrad as a major figure in British literature. Bradbrook divides Conrad's works into early (*Almayer's Folly* to "Typhoon"), mature (*Nostromo* to *Victory*), and declining (*The Shadow-Line* to *Suspense*) periods. She emphasizes the moral aspects of Conrad's writings and presents some important insights into his work. This book also serves as an important stepping stone for much criticism that would follow, in part because she anticipates the theory that Conrad's later works represent a decline in quality. Perhaps the most important figure in the recovery of Conrad's reputation, though, was Morton Dauwen Zabel, who, as early as his December 1940 article in the *New Republic* entitled "Conrad: Nel Mezzo de Cammin," argued that Conrad's reputation needed to be established once more on a firm foundation. Zabel then expanded upon these ideas in his well-known introduction to *The Portable Conrad* (1947). In this lengthy essay, he argued that Conrad was a novelist of moral insight, who imposed moral experience on the structure of his plots; Zabel also dealt with the psychological aspect of Conrad's writing as well as the inextricable nature of form and content in his works. The publication of Zabel's introduction to *The Portable Conrad* marked the permanent recovery of Conrad's reputation. The other crucial work to appear during this time was Albert J. Guerard's short book *Joseph Conrad* (1947). A precursor to his later work, *Joseph Conrad* focuses on issues that would occupy much of Conrad criticism for decades: Conrad's skepticism, his psychological investigations, and what many came to see as a strong decline in the quality of Conrad's later works. To be sure, Guerard was influenced by Morf, Zabel, Bradbrook, Crankshaw, and others, but his short book and Zabel's introduction were the strongest contribution to Conrad scholarship to date and helped to fix Conrad's reputation as one of the finest British novelists of the twentieth century. The following year F. R. Leavis, in *The Great Tradition: George Eliot, Henry James, Joseph Conrad* (1948), places Conrad among the great writers of British literature because of his moral realism and together with Zabel and Guerard effectively ends the debate concerning Conrad's place in British letters. Leavis's extended discussions of Conrad's most well-known works would influence most critics who followed him, and he continued the work of Guerard and Bradbrook in delineating canonical and non-canonical works in the Conrad opus, a trend that would continue for decades in which most critics valued most highly the works of Conrad's middle period and generally dismissed the later works and to a lesser extent the early works as well.

The 1950s was the period of Conrad's great revival. The decade began with Guerard's insightful introduction to the Signet edition of *"Heart of Darkness" & "The Secret Sharer,"* in which he outlines many of the standard views of these works such as the doubling in "The Secret Sharer" and the journey within in "Heart of Darkness." Also that year, Robert Penn Warren published his famous lengthy introduction to the Modern Library edition of *Nostromo* and discussed a number of Conrad's works alongside *Nostromo*, arguing that Conrad is a philosophical novelist in his depiction of "the black inward abyss of himself and the black outward abyss of nature." Douglas

Hewitt's book *Conrad: A Reassessment* (1952) was yet another important work that further helped to solidify Conrad's re-emergence as one of the century's most important British novelists by showing how the settings and structure of Conrad's novels helped, among other things, to present powerful representations of his central characters' inner struggles, as these struggles are considered in light of ideas of fidelity, courage, and codes of conduct and often result in a "choice of nightmares." As had Bradbrook and Guerard, Hewitt also questions the quality of Conrad's work after *Under Western Eyes*. In contrast to Hewitt, Guerard, and Bradbrook, Paul L. Wiley, in his *Conrad's Measure of Man* (1954), argues that Conrad's works fall into distinct periods that deal with different aspects of the human experience in the modern world – the early works being characterized by "hermits" or individuals isolated from society, the middle works by "incendiaries" or individuals in struggle with society, and the later works by "knights" or individuals attempting (though typically tragically) to act as rescuers. Wiley's arguments and analysis are effective, and the book remains useful, particularly as the first work to reject the idea of Conrad's declining abilities in his later works. In the area of biography, Jocelyn Baines's *Joseph Conrad: A Critical Biography* (1959) is the first good biography of Conrad and is a work that has remained useful, despite the publication of other biographies that have superseded it. Baines's is a literary biography and reads Conrad's life through his works and his works through his life, and as such set the standard for such studies.

The latter part of the decade marked the publication of three of the most important contributions in Conrad criticism to that time: Irving Howe's lengthy chapter on Conrad's politics in his *Politics and the Novel* (1957), Thomas C. Moser's *Joseph Conrad: Achievement and Decline* (1957), and Guerard's *Conrad the Novelist* (1958). Howe delineates Conrad's distaste for politics and particularly for revolutionary politics. He reads Conrad as a political conservative emphasizing his desire for order and social stability. Howe's was the first extended look at Conrad's politics. Moser's chief contribution is his theory of achievement and decline. He argues that Conrad's creative abilities declined after 1912 and that this decline resulted from his increased focus on issues of romantic love, further arguing that many of the flaws of Conrad's earlier works also involve Conrad's depiction of romance. In particular, Moser identifies issues of fidelity and betrayal as central to Conrad's best works. Similarly, he sees moral interests as informing Conrad's best works, rather than the idea of chance that appears in most of Conrad's later works. Finally, Moser's readings of Conrad's individual works are usually insightful and have been enormously influential. Even today, many Conrad scholars tend to agree with Moser's view of achievement and decline.

Guerard, by contrast, does not offer such an overarching theory regarding Conrad's works. He does work from a psychological perspective, both Jungian and Freudian, but his reading of Conrad is not reductive. In particular, Guerard emphasizes the moral challenges of Conrad's characters and their attempts at self-knowledge, highlighting their struggles to come to terms with the enigma of human existence. As he did in *Joseph Conrad*, Guerard argues for a decline in Conrad's creative powers after *Under Western Eyes*, excepting only *The Shadow-Line*. *Conrad the Novelist*'s great strength is in its readings of individual works. Many of the standard views concerning "Heart of Darkness," *Lord Jim*, and *The Nigger of the "Narcissus*," for instance, first appear in Guerard's book, and many later critical works merely expand upon issues that Guerard raises. Nearly fifty years after their publication, Moser's and Guerard's books remain standard works of Conrad criticism, and, whether one agrees or disagrees with their conclusions, one must nevertheless take them into account when studying Conrad's works.

The 1960s brought several important studies of Conrad's works, particularly regarding the politics of his novels. In 1963, Eloise Knapp Hay published *The Political Novels of Joseph Conrad* and in 1967 Avrom Fleishman published *Conrad's Politics: Community and Anarchy in the Fiction of Joseph Conrad*. These works, together with Howe's earlier treatment of the topic, shifted focus away from primarily apolitical issues, and for decades it seemed that the political world of Conrad's fiction was divided between Hay and Fleishman. Hay certainly focuses on Conrad's overtly political fiction, but she also sees Conrad's political ideas informing all of his fiction in one way or another. She argues that because of Conrad's background, politics infused all of his thinking, and thus his political ideas are a part of the very essence of Conrad's philosophy of life. As to Conrad's politics specifically, like Howe, she takes perhaps the more commonly accepted view of the time: that Conrad was fairly conservative in his politics, rejecting revolutionary activities and siding with the political establishment. On the other hand, Fleishman's important book argues that such a view oversimplifies the intellectual context and tradition in which Conrad wrote, and he sees Conrad as far less conservative than had usually been thought. Along with clearly placing Conrad within the context of both his Polish political heritage and his English and European historical and political context, Fleishman achieves a generally convincing argument regarding Conrad's political views. In addition, he provides strong readings of Conrad's works, especially regarding the need for establishing community and eschewing anarchy.

Two important biographical works also appeared during the 1960s. Norman Sherry published the first of his biographical/historical studies,

Conrad's Eastern World (1966), in which he traces the various biographical and historical sources and materials relevant to Conrad's works. Jerry Allen's biography, *The Sea Years of Joseph Conrad* (1965), had also provided some useful evidence for sources for some of Conrad's works and in this way anticipated Sherry's work, but Sherry's work overshadows Allen's. Although not infallible, *Conrad's Eastern World* remains mandatory for biographical/ historical criticism of Conrad's works. Another important biographical contribution was Bernard C. Meyer's *Joseph Conrad: A Psychoanalytic Biography* (1967). Although somewhat dated and heavily influenced by Freud, Meyer's biography is nevertheless an important addition to Conrad studies in that he links Conrad's life and personal psychology to an interpretation of his works and, if approached with some skepticism, it can still be a useful book.

A particularly important shorter work also appeared about this time. J. Hillis Miller, in a chapter on Conrad in his *Poets of Reality: Six Twentieth-Century Writers* (1965), argues for a pessimistic world view in Conrad's works that almost reaches the point of nihilism, suggesting that Conrad periodically reveals brief glimpses of the bleak truth of an irrational universe that is typically hidden from most individuals. Miller is particularly good in his discussion of *The Secret Agent*, and his views would engender an entire school of thought that saw Conrad approaching nihilism.

Another important development during this period was an increased attention to Conrad's shorter fiction. Edward W. Said published his first extended commentary on Conrad in *Joseph Conrad and the Fiction of Autobiography* (1966). It was also the first extended commentary on Conrad's short fiction. Said argues that a key to understanding Conrad's fiction comes through understanding his autobiographical writings, particularly his letters. In effect, Conrad rewrote his life in his fictional works, particularly his short fiction. In the process of his argument, Said singles out such stories as "The Secret Sharer," "The Planter of Malata," and especially *The Shadow-Line* as representing Conrad's life. Said's book concludes with *The Shadow-Line*, suggesting that it is the culmination of all Conrad's previous attempts to write his life into his fiction and represents a kind of coming to terms with himself. In the process of arguing these points, Said's argument runs counter to the achievement and decline school of thought. Following Said's lead, Lawrence Graver's *Conrad's Short Fiction* (1969) also focuses on Conrad's stories and like Said emphasizes the quality of the short fiction over the long fiction. Unlike Said, however, Graver sees a clear decline in the quality of Conrad's works. In fact, he sees a decline beginning as early as 1903.

Rounding out the decade, John A. Palmer published *Joseph Conrad's Fiction: A Study in Literary Growth* (1968), which seeks to shift the focus in

Conrad criticism away from psychological and philosophical issues and onto moral issues. Palmer also argues against a decline in Conrad's later works, suggesting instead three distinct periods in Conrad's development, each with a time of apprenticeship moving to full realization, the last period culminating in *Victory*. Of Conrad's last works, Palmer argues that rather than suffering from fatigue or a decline in his artistic abilities, these works instead suffer from the negative effects of nostalgia (*The Rover* and *The Arrow of Gold*), complicated composition (*The Rescue*), or incompleteness (*Suspense*). After Wiley's *Conrad's Measure of Man*, Palmer's is the first direct and extended response to the achievement and decline theory.

Like the 1960s, the 1970s were a particularly important time in Conrad criticism in that they introduced many of the most important debates that continue to have currency today. One of the most important of these was the debate over colonialism in Conrad. This issue came to the forefront of Conrad criticism with the publication of Chinua Achebe's "An Image of Africa" in *The Massachusetts Review* in 1977, in which he argued that Conrad's portrayal of Africans in "Heart of Darkness" was racist and that because he represents Africans as less than human the story should not be considered a great work of literature. There has probably been no more influential essay written in Conrad criticism in that this short essay has engendered countless responses. Robert F. Lee had introduced the issue of colonialism in his *Conrad's Colonialism* (1969), but he did not criticize colonial practice, nor did he consider the issue from the point of the colonized. In contrast, Achebe forever forced Conrad scholars to consider Conrad's stance on issues of race and imperialism. From the very beginning, critics have argued both for and against Achebe. Two important responses of the time were Francis B. Singh's "The Colonialist Bias in *Heart of Darkness*," which appeared in *Conradiana* in 1978, and Hunt Hawkins's "Conrad's Critique of Imperialism in *Heart of Darkness*," which appeared in *PMLA* in 1979. Although not entirely agreeing with Achebe, Singh does agree that African culture is represented as inferior in Conrad's story. In contrast, Hawkins argues that rather than being a racist who accepted colonialism, Conrad actually argues against racism and colonialism. As yet, no one seems to feel that the debate has been settled, since commentaries on the subject continue to appear with regularity.

Two important biographical works also appeared in the 1970s. First, Norman Sherry published *Conrad's Western World* (1971), a companion to his earlier *Conrad's Eastern World* and a similarly mandatory book. Later, Frederick R. Karl published his lengthy and important biography of Conrad, *Joseph Conrad: The Three Lives* (1979). Karl does not so much reinterpret Conrad's life as provide a great deal of documentation. He works from much new material in considering both Conrad's life and his works, and for a time this book took a place next to Baines's book as one of the most important biographies of Conrad.

The 1970s also saw a number of other important Conrad studies appear. The first was Bruce Johnson's *Conrad's Models of Mind* (1971), which deals with Conrad's struggle to find identity in a meaningless world. Johnson argues that Conrad approaches his fiction with certain psychological and philosophical models in mind that change over time. In particular, he sees Conrad moving from a will–passion model in his earliest writings to an ego–sympathy model. He also sees Conrad as a proto-Existentialist. Johnson's book is strongest in his discussion of Conrad's early works, and his is the first extended philosophical approach to Conrad's works since Bancroft's *Joseph Conrad: His Philosophy of Life* and as such initiated the steady stream of philosophical approaches that have appeared since. That same year, Royal Roussel published *The Metaphysics of Darkness: A Study in the Unity and Development of Conrad's Fiction.* Influenced by the ideas of J. Hillis Miller, Roussel argues that Conrad's fiction confronts what Roussel calls "the darkness," the force at the heart of Conrad's universe. He discusses three stages in Conrad's works: the first shows writing as a possible way to place oneself in the material world; the second reveals Conrad believing less and less in the visible world; and the third sees him trying to find identity through commitment to the world. Unlike the philosophical studies of Johnson and Roussel, David Thorburn, in *Conrad's Romanticism* (1974), revisits the issue of Romanticism in Conrad's works. Walter F. Wright, in *Romance and Tragedy in Joseph Conrad* (1949), Ruth M. Stauffer, in *Joseph Conrad: His Romantic-Realism* (1922), and Walpole, in *Joseph Conrad*, had addressed the idea of Romanticism in Conrad's works, but unlike them Thorburn argues that Conrad was really more of a nineteenth-century author than a twentieth-century author, suggesting that he had much in common with writers such as Rudyard Kipling and Robert Louis Stevenson. Thorburn further argues that many of the elements in Conrad's fiction result from Romantic ideas, and he even proposes the influence of English Romantic lyric poetry on Conrad. Thorburn presents a corrective to those who would see Conrad only in terms of Modernism. In contrast, C. B. Cox, in his *Joseph Conrad: The Modern Imagination* (1974), argues that Conrad is solely a writer of the twentieth century, suggesting that Conrad engages nihilism and is a proto-Existentialist. Cox sees Conrad bringing together alienation and commitment in his works, which results in indeterminacy. H. M. Daleski takes up a different issue in his *Joseph Conrad: The Way of Dispossession* (1977), which, as the title suggests, sees the dispossession of the self as a central issue in Conrad's works. Daleski argues that one must be in possession of the self in order to demonstrate virtues such as fidelity, and when one loses possession of the self, one is destroyed, either physically or spiritually. Daleski also argues, though, that ultimately self-possession often can result only from consciously letting go of one's self and thus coming to a greater awareness of self. Another work in some ways concerned with the self is Jeremy Hawthorn's *Joseph Conrad: Language and Fictional Self-Consciousness* (1979), which argues that Conrad's works are always self-referential. Hawthorn focuses particularly on language, and, influenced by linguistic and Marxist theory, he argues for a relationship between the subjective and objective through language, suggesting that language is the means by which subjective experience can be translated into objective experience. Ian Watt concludes the 1970s, and fittingly so; his *Conrad in the Nineteenth Century* (1979) has taken a place next to Moser's and Guerard's books as a standard work of Conrad criticism. Part formalist, part biographical/historicist, part intellectual historicist, Watt's unique blend of approaches provides for an intelligent reading of Conrad. His extended discussions of Conrad's technique of delayed decoding and his views on Conrad's relationship to Impressionism and Symbolism have become standard views in Conrad scholarship. Furthermore, Watt's clear and reasoned readings have influenced many who followed him.

The 1980s continued many of the debates that arose in previous decades, expanding and augmenting them. In addition, a number of studies informed by poststructural literary theory also appeared during this time. The first of these is William W. Bonney's *Thorns & Arabesques: Contexts for Conrad's Fiction* (1980), which follows in the tradition of Miller and Roussel and argues for a kind of nihilism in Conrad's works. Informed by contemporary literary theory, Bonney argues that a tension exists in Conrad's works that results in both construction and de-construction of certain ideas. Bonney suggests that Conrad affirms discontinuity, deconstructs the Romance, and engages in various forms of linguistic discontinuity. Fredric Jameson's chapter on Conrad in his *The Political Unconscious* (1981) is also influenced by poststructural thought, as well as by Marxist thought. In this influential commentary, Jameson looks at the ideas of Romance and reification in Conrad's writings, particularly in *Lord Jim* and *Nostromo*, arguing that Conrad's works represent a fault line in modern literature in which the literary and cultural structures become visible in a way they were not previously. Aaron Fogel's important *Coercion to Speak: Conrad's Poetics of Dialogue* (1985) moves in a somewhat different direction and approaches Conrad's works in light of Mikhail Bakhtin's theories. Fogel focuses largely on Conrad's political novels and looks at the ways characters speak to one another, or more particularly the ways they force others to speak. Fogel sees coerced speech as a major feature of Conrad's works. Similarly informed by post-structural thought, Suresh Ravel's *The Art of Failure: Conrad's Fiction* (1986) considers Conrad's skepticism toward language and fiction, which leads to despair at achieving ultimate understanding and also leads to dilemmas in human social and political life. Ravel argues that throughout Conrad's works, opposing ideas exist and intermingle, resulting in philosophical complexity and demonstrating the ultimate indeterminacy of any definitive conclusions to the issues raised. Somewhat different from these other theoretically informed studies, Jakob Lothe's *Conrad's Narrative Method* (1989) is more eclectic and is informed by structuralism, narratology, and other contemporary literary theory. Lothe disputes the idea that content precedes form in fiction and in that light investigates Conrad's narrative methodology. Lothe discusses Conrad's narrative methodology itself as well as the relationship between narrative and thematics in Conrad's works.

Along with poststructural approaches, issues of postcolonialism appeared during this time. Following the lead of Achebe, Singh, Hawkins, and others, John A. McClure's *Kipling and Conrad: The Colonial Fiction* (1981) looks at the works of Kipling and Conrad in relation to the issue of colonialism, arguing in particular that both writers challenged Romantic ideas about colonialism. McClure also looks at their differing responses to the topic, suggesting that while Kipling often looked for ways to improve the colonial system, Conrad saw little to redeem it. Similarly, Benita Parry's *Conrad and Imperialism: Ideological Boundaries and Visionary Frontiers* (1983) considers issues of colonialism in Conrad's fiction. Parry's work is particularly informed by Marxist theory, and she argues that on the one hand Conrad affirms certain aspects of European imperialism, while at the same time critiquing it.

In addition to poststructural and postcolonial commentaries, other important studies appeared during this time. Following Wiley and Palmer, Gary Geddes's *Conrad's Later Novels* (1980) is a defense of Conrad's later fiction in which he argues that Conrad attempts something different in his later fiction. Unlike the psychological dramas of his earlier works, Conrad focuses on Romance and symbol in his later works. Geddes sees Conrad as a skeptical Humanist in these works, with the concept of the rescue predominating them. In particular, Geddes sees the value of Conrad's later works in the ironic Romances he wrote. Similarly, Daniel R. Schwarz's *Conrad: The Later Fiction* (1982) also rejects the achievement and decline theory of Conrad's career. Though formalist in method and Humanist in idea, Schwarz works less from an overarching thesis than from analyses of individual works. In particular, he defends the quality of Conrad's later fiction and argues against Moser's criticism of the love relationships in the later works. The groundwork laid by Wiley, Palmer, Geddes, and Schwarz lead to much of the debate over the achievement and decline theory that exists today.

As for biographical works, Zdzisław Najder's *Joseph Conrad: A Chronicle* (1983), was, and it still is, the single most important biography on Conrad. Having access to materials in Polish as well as those in French and English along with his close reliance on document evidence, Najder was able to give a more complete picture of Conrad than had previously been possible. Furthermore, his strict reliance on documentation results in a minimum of speculation.

Continuing the trend begun largely in the 1980s, a number of works that appeared in the 1990s proceed from poststructural and other contemporary literary theory. Informed by contemporary narrative theory, Jeremy Hawthorn's *Joseph Conrad: Narrative Technique and Ideological Commitment* (1990) looks at the relationship between form and content in Conrad's works, arguing that the two are inextricably intertwined in Conrad's most successful works. In fact, Hawthorn suggests that the disjunction between the two signals Conrad's failed literary efforts. Similarly, poststructural theory informs Daphna Erdinast-Vulcan's *Joseph Conrad and the Modern Temper* (1991), as she sees Conrad responding to the Modernist view of the world. In particular, she looks at Conrad's affinities with Nietzsche's view of the world and focuses heavily on a conflict in Conrad's fiction between his wish to believe in values but his inability to do so. Working from a different poststructural background, Bruce Henricksen's *Nomadic Voices: Conrad and the Subject of Narrative* (1992) proceeds from the views of Bakhtin and Jean-François Lyotard and argues that Conrad's works move from monologic in *The Nigger of the "Narcissus"* to polyphonic in *Under Western Eyes*. In the process, Henricksen takes issue with Fogel's *Coercion to Speak* and looks at the opposing individual and political views in Conrad's texts as manifestations of the dialogic quality of those works. In the same way, he sees the problem of the modern fragmented self in the various "nomadic" voices that appear in Conrad's works. Poststructural thought also runs in the background of Geoffrey Galt Harpham's *One of Us: The Mastery of Joseph Conrad* (1996), in which he considers the "three lives" of Karl's biography, that is Conrad's life as a youth in Poland, as a mariner at sea, and as a writer in England, but not as separate and consecutive entities but rather as a kind of simultaneity, looking at the way Conrad both mastered and was mastered by the environment in which he existed. Similarly, working from a background in contemporary literary theory, in *The Strange Short Fiction of Joseph Conrad: Writing, Culture and Subjectivity* (1999), Daphna Erdinast-Vulcan both follows upon and diverges from her earlier book. Influenced by Jacques Derrida and Bakhtin, Erdinast-Vulcan considers the problems of the author and subjectivity in Conrad's short fiction. In particular, she argues that Conrad's Romanticism and Modernism can be linked to Postmodernism such that Conrad's works exhibit relationships between metaphysics and subjectivity, between subjectivity and inter-subjectivity, and between psychology and textuality, as well as evidencing a wish for subjective aesthetization.

Although the issue of women in Conrad dates at least as far back as Colbrun's 1914 essay, it is a topic that had been largely ignored, except for some occasional essays on the subject. Ruth L. Nadelhaft's *Joseph Conrad* (1991) is the first extended study of Conrad and his works in light of feminist theory. In particular, Nadelhaft argues that Conrad's female characters have a much greater role in Conrad's fiction than has usually been assumed. Following Nadelhaft's lead, Susan Jones, in *Conrad and Women* (1999), argues that contrary to long-accepted tradition, Conrad is not a man's author but rather that women strongly influenced his writing, that women characters often serve crucial roles in his fiction, and that Conrad usually had women particularly in mind as his reading public. She suggests that this fact was especially true of Conrad's later career. In the process of her argument, Jones also rejects the achievement and decline view of Conrad's career. Both Nadelhaft and Jones opened up the issue of women in Conrad's works and pointed the way to a new and now expanding direction for Conrad studies.

The continuing interest in postcolonial studies in general during this time also appears extensively in Conrad studies. These writers, of course, follow in the footsteps of such earlier commentators as Achebe, McClure, Parry, and others, and each considers different aspects of the issue. Chris Bongie's *Exotic Memories: Literature, Colonialism, and the* Fin de Siècle (1991) argues that the exoticism that some writers at the turn of the twentieth century looked toward was in essence already a thing of the past. Bongie suggests that in "Heart of Darkness" Conrad argues for a tension between criticizing and rationalizing colonialism, and of Conrad's other colonial works, Bongie argues that contrary to nineteenth-century exoticism Conrad represents an exoticism devoid of the sharp distinctions between primitive and civilized. On the other hand, Andrea White's *Joseph Conrad and the Adventure Tradition: Constructing and Deconstructing the Imperial Subject* (1993) considers the nineteenth-century adventure tradition and uses Conrad's works before 1900 to argue that he admired the discoveries and accomplishments of that tradition while at the same time rejecting much of the imperialist baggage that came with it. Christopher GoGwilt's *The Invention of the West: Joseph Conrad and the Double-Mapping of Europe and Empire* (1995) is one of the more important works in this area. Going back to the very heart of the distinctions between East and West, he argues that the idea of a unified West was one that was constructed in order to dominate the non-Western world. GoGwilt considers Conrad's view of the West and suggests that he vacillates between supporting and rejecting the idea of the West as it had been constructed.

Several other important studies appeared in the 1990s. Yves Hervouet's *The French Face of Joseph Conrad* (1990) considers the influence of French literature on Conrad's works. Hervouet discusses Conrad's knowledge of French authors as well as the literary, aesthetic, and philosophical influence of specific writers on Conrad's fiction. Although Conrad's Polish background had long been the study of scholars, no one before had extensively considered the significant influence of French literature and culture on Conrad's development. In the area of philosophical approaches, Mark A. Wollaeger's *Joseph Conrad and the Fictions of Skepticism* (1990) considers Conrad's skepticism in light of a tradition of philosophical skepticism descending from René Descartes to Stanley Cavell. In particular, Wollaeger argues for a dialogical tension between competing ideas in Conrad's fiction, specifically between skepticism and attempts to resist the consequences of skepticism. Similarly, although others had previously argued for Existential elements in Conrad's works, Otto Bohlmann's *Conrad's Existentialism* (1991) thoroughly investigates the issue and argues for Conrad as a proto-Existentialist, considering Conrad's works in light of a number of Existentialist thinkers, including Jean-Paul Sartre, Albert Camus, Søren Kierkegaard, Nietzsche, Gabriel Marcel, and others. In particular, he looks at the ideas of Being in the world, the quest for selfhood, condemned to be free, and Being with others.

The turn of the twenty-first century has not witnessed a slackening of interest in Conrad studies. While many other traditionally canonical authors receive less and less attention, interest in Conrad seems to be burgeoning, as evidenced by the number of important Conrad studies that have already appeared. For instance, Peter Edgerly Firchow's *Envisioning Africa: Racism and Imperialism in Conrad's* Heart of Darkness (2000) jumps into the fray regarding Conrad and colonialism and sets out to defend him against Achebe's charges of racism. Firchow argues that Achebe misunderstands Conrad, and he suggests that Conrad sought to represent not Africa but rather an image of Africa. Firchow further argues that issues of race and imperialism had a different meaning in Conrad's time from now and that Conrad should be judged in the context of his own time. Similarly, Robert

Hampson's *Cross-Cultural Encounters in Joseph Conrad's Malay Fiction* (2000) works with new historicist, postcolonial, and postmodern theory to argue that Conrad's writing about the Malay Archipelago resulted both from his own experience and from a Western construction of Malaysia. Hampson suggests that Conrad recognized this cultural construction and consistently undermined it. In the process, Hampson identifies the problems with Western attempts to inscribe non-Western cultures. Augmenting this discussion, Stephen Ross, in his *Conrad and Empire* (2004), works from contemporary theoretical ideas and argues that Conrad's interest in imperialism is only part of a larger concern with the problem of globalization. He sees Conrad's novels confronting a global capitalism that has replaced the traditional concept of nation-state and demonstrates the effects of such a change on the individuals that populate his fiction.

In addition to postcolonial issues, poststructural issues have continued to play a prominent role in Conrad studies. Andrew Michael Roberts's *Conrad and Masculinity* (2000) considers contemporary issues of gender in light of poststructural theory, as he looks at masculinity in Conrad and views it as a cultural construct, arguing that Conrad both represents and at the same time questions this construct. In the process, he also argues for links between masculinity and imperialism, feminism, and homoeroticism. In another use of poststructural theory, Michael Greaney's *Conrad, Language, and Narrative* (2002) focuses on the ideas of speech and narrative. Influenced by Derrida and Bakhtin, Greaney suggests that a tension exists between speech and writing in Conrad's works. To this end, he argues for three phases of narrative development. The first that occurs is storytelling in the oral or communal mode that appears in the early Malay fiction. This mode evolves into a second phase, represented by the Marlow narratives, in which a tension develops between authentic and inauthentic language. Finally, a third mode appears in the political novels in which storytelling gives way to Modernist aesthetics. Also looking at language and Modernity, but from a different angle, Con Coroneos, in *Space, Conrad, and Modernity* (2002), is especially influenced by the ideas of Michel Foucault and considers the relationship between space and Modernity, using Conrad as a kind of touchstone for his discussion. In particular, he is interested in the opposition between a space of things and a space of words. To this end, he considers the idea of closed space and argues that language (one of the book's major concerns) is a means of escaping the limitations of closed space.

Other twenty-first-century studies of Conrad's works include my own *Conrad and Impressionism* (2001) and Martin Bock's *Joseph Conrad and Psychological Medicine* (2002). *Conrad and Impressionism* is a philosophical study that argues that an Impressionist epistemology runs throughout Conrad's works and manifests itself in his narrative techniques. This epistemology results from Conrad's skepticism regarding the ability of human beings to know anything with certainty. Consequently, a link exists between Conrad's literary technique, philosophical presuppositions, and socio-political views. On the other hand, as the title suggests, *Joseph Conrad and Psychological Medicine* is a psychological study that argues for applying pre-Freudian medical psychology when looking at the physical and mental illnesses in Conrad's life and works and suggesting that Conrad's works consistently deal with various forms of mental illness, particularly hysteria, and that such issues as seclusion, restraint, and water, which appear prominently in Conrad's works, come from contemporary medical views of the time. Two other recent books consider areas of Conrad studies that previously had received little attention. Richard J. Hand, in *The Theatre of Joseph Conrad: Reconstructed Fictions* (2005), argues that Conrad's plays are worth studying. Hand looks at Conrad's drama in light of the well-made play and contemporary melodrama, while also arguing that these plays look forward to Theatre of the Absurd and contain overtones of Grand-Guignol, Symbolism, and Expressionism. In a different direction, Stephen Donovan's *Joseph Conrad and Popular Culture* (2005) reconsiders the idea that Conrad scorned popular culture, arguing instead that although Conrad often did look down upon popular culture, his works are filled with references to the popular culture of the time. Donovan further argues that one can gain a greater understanding of Conrad's works by understanding the popular culture in which he wrote.

The sheer number of books that have been written and continue to be written on this unique literary figure attests to Conrad's place in twentieth-century British literature and to his interest to students of literature today.

Guide to further reading

What follows is a brief list of works that would be particularly useful to students. Naturally, much of what is contained in Chapter 6 would also be valuable to students, but this Guide to further reading focuses specifically on works that would be accessible to and appropriate for undergraduate and graduate students. Included are both primary and secondary works.

Primary texts

Conrad's writings

Conrad, Joseph. *The Cambridge Edition of the Works of Joseph Conrad.* 3 vols. to date. Cambridge: Cambridge University Press, 1990–
    The Cambridge editions are considered authoritative editions of Conrad's works. Only three volumes, however, have been published at this point in time.

Conrad, Joseph. *The Complete Works of Joseph Conrad.* 26 vols. Garden City, NY: Doubleday, Page & Co., 1926.
    In the United States, the Doubleday edition, often called the Uniform edition, is the standard edition where the Cambridge edition is not available.

Conrad, Joseph. *The Collected Edition of the Works of Joseph Conrad.* 22 vols. London: J. M. Dent & Sons, 1946–55.
    In the United Kingdom, the Dent collected edition is generally considered the standard edition where the Cambridge edition is not available.

Conrad's letters

Conrad, Joseph. *The Collected Letters of Joseph Conrad,* ed. Frederick R. Karl, Laurence Davies, J. H. Stape, and Owen Knowles. 7 vols. to date. Cambridge: Cambridge University Press, 1983–

The Cambridge University Press edition of Conrad's letters is the most
authoritative edition, but it is not quite complete, covering letters to 1922.

Jean-Aubry, G. *Joseph Conrad: Life and Letters.* 2 vols. Garden City, NY:
Doubleday, Page & Co., 1927.
For Conrad's letters of 1923 and 1924, Jean-Aubry's edition is probably the
best.

Secondary texts

Commentary

Achebe, Chinua. "An Image of Africa." *Massachusetts Review* 18.4 (winter 1977):
782–94.
The essay that began the still ongoing discussion concerning Conrad's
relationship to colonialism and argues that Conrad's portrayal of Africans is
racist.

Berthoud, Jacques. *Joseph Conrad: The Major Phase.* Cambridge: Cambridge
University Press, 1978.
A good overview with solid and clear discussions of Conrad's works in light of
Conrad's own views of art.

Carabine, Keith, ed. *Joseph Conrad: Critical Assessments.* 4 vols. Mountfield,
East Essex, England: Helm Information, 1992.
A useful collection of reviews and articles about Conrad's works.

Daleski, H. M. *Joseph Conrad: The Way of Dispossession.* London: Faber & Faber,
1977.
A good commentary on Conrad's works, which focuses on issues of the self.

Fleishman, Avrom. *Conrad's Politics: Community and Anarchy in the Fiction of
Joseph Conrad.* Baltimore, Md.: Johns Hopkins University Press, 1967.
A good discussion of Conrad's politics, which argues for Conrad as a more
liberal political thinker than what had usually been assumed, somewhat
challenging but nevertheless accessible.

Gillon, Adam. *Joseph Conrad.* Boston: Twayne Publishers, 1982.
A useful overview of Conrad's works, which emphasizes Conrad's Polish
background.

Guerard, Albert J. *Conrad the Novelist.* Cambridge, Mass.: Harvard University
Press, 1958.
A standard work of Conrad studies with well-argued readings of Conrad's
works.

Gurko, Leo. *Joseph Conrad: Giant in Exile.* New York: Macmillan Publishing Co.,
1962.
A helpful general commentary on Conrad's works.

Hay, Eloise Knapp. *The Political Novels of Joseph Conrad: A Critical Study.*
Chicago: University of Chicago Press, 1963.

A good commentary on Conrad's politics, which tends to see Conrad as a
    political conservative.
Hewitt, Douglas. *Conrad: A Reassessment.* Cambridge: Bowes & Bowes
    Publishers, 1952.
    A standard work of Conrad studies, which argues for the quality of Conrad's
    works at a time in which his reputation was still in question.
Jones, Susan. *Conrad and Women.* Oxford: Clarendon Press, 1999.
    A very good commentary on women in Conrad's works.
Karl, Frederick R. *A Reader's Guide to Joseph Conrad*, rev. edn. New York: Farrar,
    Straus & Giroux, 1969.
    A good general overview of Conrad's works, although many works are
    dismissed out of hand.
Knowles, Owen and Gene M. Moore. *Oxford Reader's Companion to Conrad.*
    Oxford: Oxford University Press, 2000.
    A fine reference book to Conrad's life and works.
Leavis, F. R. *The Great Tradition: George Eliot, Henry James, Joseph Conrad.*
    New York: George W. Stewart, Publisher [1948].
    This book contains an important chapter that argues that Conrad was a major
    figure in a great tradition of English novelists.
Miller, J. Hillis. *Poets of Reality: Six Twentieth-Century Writers.* Cambridge, Mass.:
    Harvard University Press, 1965.
    This book contains an influential chapter on Conrad that emphasizes
    Conrad's philosophical skepticism.
Moore, Gene M., ed. *Conrad on Film.* Cambridge: Cambridge University Press,
    1997.
    A good collection of essays on the filming of Conrad's works.
Moser, Thomas C. *Joseph Conrad: Achievement and Decline.* Cambridge, Mass.:
    Harvard University Press, 1957.
    A standard work in Conrad studies, which argues for an artistic decline in
    Conrad's later works, largely as a result of his emphasis on romance in those
    works.
Nadelhaft, Ruth L. *Joseph Conrad.* Atlantic Highlands, NJ: Humanities Press
    International, 1991.
    A general overview of Conrad's works focusing on the role of women in those
    works.
Palmer, John A. *Joseph Conrad's Fiction: A Study in Literary Growth.* Ithaca, NY:
    Cornell University Press, 1968.
    A helpful discussion of Conrad's works that does not dismiss Conrad's later
    works.
Peters, John G. *Conrad and Impressionism.* Cambridge: Cambridge University
    Press, 2001.
    A look at Conrad's works in light of philosophies of knowledge.
Schwarz, Daniel R. *Conrad: "Almayer's Folly" to "Under Western Eyes."* Ithaca,
    NY: Cornell University Press, 1980.
    A useful formalist reading of Conrad's early and middle writings.

Stape, J. H., ed. *The Cambridge Companion to Joseph Conrad.* Cambridge: Cambridge University Press, 1996.
> A good collection of essays covering the major issues surrounding Conrad's works.

Warren, Robert Penn. "Introduction." *Nostromo* by Joseph Conrad. New York: The Modern Library, 1951.
> Although focusing on *Nostromo*, this is an important commentary on Conrad's works in general, particularly emphasizing the philosophical aspects of Conrad's works.

Watt, Ian. *Conrad in the Nineteenth Century.* Berkeley: University of California Press, 1979.
> A standard work of Conrad commentary, which works from a close reading of the texts and considers them in the context of their intellectual history.

Zabel, Morton Dauwen. "Introduction." *The Portable Conrad.* New York: Viking Press, 1947, 1–47.
> An important critical work on Conrad's works and one of the principle commentaries in restoring Conrad's reputation from its decline after Conrad's death, it emphasizes the moral and psychological aspects of Conrad's works.

Biographical works

Baines, Jocelyn. *Joseph Conrad: A Critical Biography.* London: Weidenfeld & Nicolson, 1959.
> A good literary biography, although it has since been superseded by the influx of Polish biographical sources.

Najder, Zdzisław. *Joseph Conrad: A Chronicle*, trans. Halina Carroll-Najder. Cambridge: Cambridge University Press, 1983.
> The best biography of Conrad.

Sherry, Norman. *Conrad's Eastern World.* Cambridge: Cambridge University Press, 1966.
> An important book, which searches for the sources for Conrad's themes and characters in his works set in the East.

Conrad's Western World. Cambridge: Cambridge University Press, 1971.
> A companion to Sherry's earlier volume, this book focuses on Conrad's works set in the West.

Bibliographies

Knowles, Owen. *An Annotated Critical Bibliography of Joseph Conrad.* New York: St. Martin's Press, 1992.
> A good, selective, annotated bibliography of commentary on Conrad's life and works through 1990.

Teets, Bruce E. *Joseph Conrad: An Annotated Bibliography.* New York: Garland
Publishing, 1990.
A useful annotated bibliography of commentary from 1965 to 1975, including
much of the commentary from 1895 until 1965 that does not appear in the
Teets and Gerber bibliography.
Teets, Bruce E. and Helmut E. Gerber. *Joseph Conrad: An Annotated Bibliography
of Writings about Him.* De Kalb, Ill.: Northern Illinois University Press, 1971.
A useful, though incomplete, annotated bibliography of commentary on
Conrad's life and works from 1895 until 1965.

Index